Heavy, Deep & Real Funny

A humorous & fresh perspective on life, loss, love and forgiveness.

By Amanda Sharp

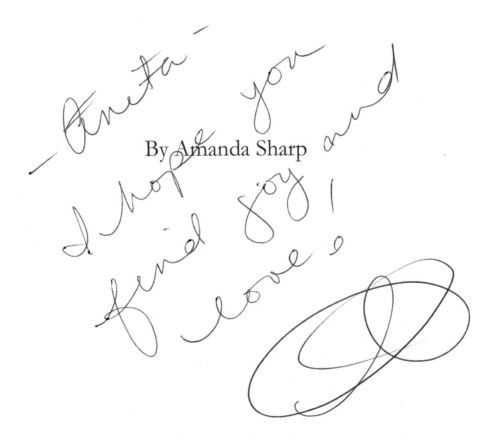

ISBN-13:
978-0692311530

ISBN-10:
069231153X

DEDICATION

To God

Thank you for giving me this book and writing it with me.
You have always spoken clearly to me when I actually create
the time to listen. Thank you for loving me so immensely & intimately.
I truly hope you are found in this by others and it brings new hope
and relationship with you. I guess I'll find out in heaven if you thought it was funny.

To my boys, my gifts, Corbyn and Tyler

Dream big and know you can do anything you desire,
especially if God is in it. You bring so much joy to my life.

AMANDA SHARP

ABOUT THE AUTHOR

Amanda was born in Boulder, Colorado and grew up in many cities with Grand Lake & Breckenridge CO being her favorites. She graduated from Denver South High School. She attended and graduated from Oral Roberts University with a major in Commercial Art (Graphic Art), was a NCAA Volleyball Player & the yearbook photographer. She is a product of divorce and quite frankly someone you'll want to know. Varied life experiences, during high school years including frequent moves, new step parents and siblings, sports, leadership, youth groups, high school clubs, and academic excellence, combined to create the person she is today. She makes and keeps friends easily and is loyal in her pursuit of relationships. She finds great joy in supporting her friends in their personal goals and dreaming again.

She is a huge fan of SHOCK humor and especially with people she perceives haven't laughed in awhile. Along the way, she was told often that she is heavy deep and real (dives into deep subjects) and has been told her whole life that her wit and humor is one of a kind. You could ask any person to describe her and humor would be one of the top three. She knows how to bring a comfort level in people and non-judgmental space that creates utmost honesty about their struggles.

She was married for 14 years and has 2 amazing and beautiful boys. Through the pain of divorce, this book was conceived. Her goal was to help her boys and herself walk through it by choosing life and humor. They are her inspiration for many laughs. (the wit and humor in the house is mind blowing for sure). Amanda is a single mom, working as a graphic artist, photographer and health and wellness coach and business mentor.

Her work with a personal development company in the last 7 years has contributed to her character development & sense of humor. Her life goals included becoming a woman of excellence in her pursuit of God. Her hopes for this, her first book is that the reader will find freedom through their suffering and release their sense of humor on their next step of their journey, creating a new outlook. She has always looked at self improvement as a must. Evolving her character, she strives to be an amazing woman of God that hopes to make a large difference in this world. She absolutely trusts that the timing will be perfect for her reader to pick this book up. It can be flipped through or read cover to cover.

She has been an avid blogger since 2009 and has attracted hundreds of readers. As a result of the feedback, she decided to compile those blogs and life adventures into this compelling, thought provoking book detailing her spiritual quest and struggle to come out of the sorrow of lost dreams that can be created by divorce. This book will be exactly that! She wants you to have an opportunity to look at your struggle in a new light and perhaps encounter God on your journey. Dig in and enjoy!

The hurdle of finishing this book for Amanda has been "Can or should a Christian be funny? The struggle between perversion, wit and sarcasm has been a life long challenge. She definitely believes she has been gifted with humor and spreading joy. With every gift you have the opposite which would be biting angry sarcasm and being a "take" or negative energy in a room. This book was written to get the reader out of their comfort zone and to find out what is true and real for them. If you struggle with having and being fun, then you might enjoy the small tall tales or other comedic pieces. You might choose to come from complete imprisonment of judgment and not shift at all. This is a journey you get to create. If you want to be funny then hang out with funny people. If you want to be a deeper thinker and work on your character then hang out with people you believe do that easily. This book is a great place to see where you are at, where you can shift and what's just not for you.

Does God have a sense of humor? Well, have you seen the naked mole rat?

Okay then, onward, surrender and have fun.

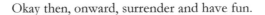

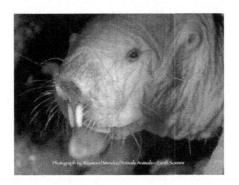

Photograph by Raymond Mendez/Animals Animals—Earth Scenes

Amanda is tired of not writing and completing this book because it might be a "turn off" to tight lipped stuffy Christians (her perception and judgment). The ones that walk in such judgment it hinders them from laughing about the craziness of life for years, even decades. How is that working for you? Do you want to be open to something different?

We are all leading people somewhere on an hourly basis with our opinions and attitudes.
"The question isn't if you are a leader, the question is: would you follow you?"
–Amanda Sharp

Please email her at sharpdesignsinc@mac.com, find her on Facebook, Twitter (sharptweetinit), Instagram (sharpdesigns), and Vine (Heavy Deep and Real Funny)

INTRODUCTION

Welcome to the place that I have wanted to create for years, maybe even decades. Now don't get comfortable cause I plan on opening up my whole being into this book. With that comes all spectrums of my personality. I am a person of great depth, a seeker of truth, an abolisher of the "elephant in the room" and finally one of the funniest people you will meet. It has taken me years to own that last sentence and it's true. I'm not claiming to be the best rocket scientist, I'm claiming something that has been on my report card since a young age. I've heard that if you hear that you are a jackass from three people then you should probably buy a saddle and ride that bad boy (own it baby). What have people told you your whole life that you are good at? This platform is my way of owning my gifts: journeying on the path laid out for me and walking through the pain and joy life brings everyone. Ultimately, my purpose is to create a space for you to relate, grow, and bring grace into your relationships. I have discovered that when I come from a personally responsible place I am more effective, vulnerable and powerful. Mostly, I am personally responsible for my actions, my responses and my truths.

You see, I believe if we would just admit that we are Full of Shizznit, then we are at a place where God can use us. It is the FOS factor. I would like you to take a moment to think about 1 time that you weren't FOS. I'm not sure I can think of one but good luck. Now I am coming from this space because I have seen God completely use me in that humble state, and quite frankly I want more of that. Who wouldn't? So what I'm going to do is take you on a journey of my heavy, deep and real funny life. I will strive to bring light to uncomfortable truths and I will, of course, bring my unique humorous outlook cause, dang it, life is hilarious. In my opinion, if you aren't laughing, you are crying.

Heck, we've all had massive loss in our lives. If I want to ride the pity train, it will take me straight down to the depths of despair. I take responsibility for what I get to create in life, and what I choose my response to be to my circumstances. I want to give you new outlooks, different ways at looking at things and by God, I hope you meet Jesus in the midst. That's really between you and Him though. Your beliefs are yours, I can't change that nor care to. I do care about abolishing some negative self talk, laugh with you, and create a space where you can lift your head and keep moving!

I have attracted funny into every day of my life quite honestly. I don't know if I would have made it through some of my trials if I didn't have this coping tool. I'm going to push raw subjects, be vulnerable, and open my whole self to your judgment in order for you to perhaps find your truth.

This could very well challenge you deeply and also in a legalistic way. I haven't written this book yet because I was in so much fear of "leading the flock astray" or being judged. I believe God is a little more powerful than that, don't you think? So here it goes. I'm going to just do it and Lord I pray that anything that is not of you falls to deaf ears and memory. I believe as a human, I bring immense laughter and love from my God and He walks through ALL with me. I do know I grieve Him as well, AND I choose to live in the grace room. When it is something I can correct or apologize for I want to. This has served me so much in the past 3-5 years.

So put on your Depends, strap down your seat belt and open your heart. On some level, as an exhausted Christian, maybe this is the key to releasing your soul from jail.

The format that lies ahead, in these pages, will be first a small tall tale or humorous outlook on life. Basically I take a story and slap some odd humor and descriptions that I hope creates laughter. What I'm really wanting to say is I'm a liar (lol) because the truth is definitely expounded on. Then a raw topic that creates space for you to think about how your are personally affected. Then you will be given an action step that you can choose in to. I highly request you choose in to the action steps so that you aren't just reading a book from a human but allowing God to speak and be with you. Also if a song is suggested, please look it up on You Tube and play it before, during or after reading the piece you are on. Music has an amazing way of getting us connected to our heart, emotions, memories and pain quickly. Last, a journaling section for you to write your Aha's, downloads from God or thoughts.

Have fun because that is one area I would love to challenge you in.

I hope to leave a legacy of Love and Laughter. Enjoy ---Amanda

She is clothed in strength and dignity and laughs without fear of the future. -Psalms 3

ACKNOWLEDGMENTS

To my God

May this book be pleasing to you as you are the only one I strive to be pleasing to.

To my boys, my gifts, Corbyn and Tyler

I am so proud of whom you are. You bring daily humor and joy to my life. I love you with all of my heart. Thank you for encouraging me to keep writing and giving me my "why" for doing things with excellence. Thank you for walking this journey and healing along side me.

To my mom, my mentor

You have been my number one fan. You have taught me all the traits of a woman of God through your actions which includes joy, laughter, forgiveness, peace and contentment. Thank you for your unconditional love. Thank you for supporting this project as well and taking the time to read over it with love and prayer. It is a true gift to have your healthy mentorship for a lifetime. I am the woman I am today because of your Godly leading.

Oh, and thank you for pushing me out that cold winter day.

Jen, my late step-sister

Thank you for being my biggest fan around this book and encouraging me to keep writing. I was so honored when you told me you wanted to edit it and be a part of it. It grieves me that you passed away before this could happen, and I know you are looking down on me with a huge smile and a proud heart for me to complete this. This is for us girl!

To Destiny

Thank you for offering to take the reins and edit this book with love and support. Your friendship is extremely valuable to me and I truly appreciate you for supporting me in an area I lack.

To many family & friends

Thank you for always standing in the gap and creating the space for me to be the best person I can. I have laughed my whole life and have had amazingly deep relationships that have rounded me into whom I was created to be. There are at least 50 people that come to mind. Please know you have all been extremely valuable to my growth and stepping into my calling. You may just find yourself in my writings. Thank you to those who wrote excerpts for my testimonials.

AMANDA SHARP

IN THE BEGINNING

It was a cold and windy day. Dianne was truly thankful she made it to the hospital in time as she huffed and puffed, fogging up the car windows. Well, in time meaning, she didn't push me out in the back seat of the odd smelling, musty, lime green pleather seat of our 63 Dodge Dart. Dianne had been doing her kegels the best she knew how and even that wasn't helping. She had been with this baby for 9 months and already understood that it had quite the personality. She could feel at times the fetus laughing inside, almost like it had already found plenty to laugh about. This is the real definition of "inside jokes." She was scared because this personality was passed down from a long lineage of humorous women that straddled the line of Godly and extremely inappropriate. Be very clear it got worse as the women got louder and more outspoken through the generations.

So as I was deciding when to come out, cause you know it was up to me; I was trying to figure out a stellar way of doing it. Should I bang my head up against the pelvic bone for 3 hours and completely deform my head in the canal? Should I bungee jump with the umbilical cord and do a peak-a-boo appearance as I pop in and out slipping in and out of the doctors grasp? Should I wait until the forceps come up and clench my cranium and crack a few bones? Don't worry they grow back, it just might cause a cowlick that will only look good with a mullet style haircut. Or should I be really unthankful and wait for the knife to cut through and move all my mom's organs to the side so they can bring me into this world? Hmmmm decisions.

I finally decide to make my appearance through the birth canal, the fun and easy way. Why not "slip my mom a solid" and give her a memory that brings a smile to her face. I was going to still play dead for a couple minutes just to see if they really wanted me. As the pelvic walls clench down on my body I get moved inch by inch down the birth canal. Each advance is making a nice indention on my body kind of like the ones on a can of cranberry sauce. I can hear my mom's heartbeat and also her whiney screaming as if this is a problem for her. Suddenly everything relaxes and I retreat into a state of bliss as I grab a pelvic bone and move myself clear of this large needle coming through my mom's spine. Ahhhh, everything is calm again.

I ponder what its going to be like out there and who I am going to be. I make a promise to myself to be the greatest me I can be. I promise to be a truth seeker and I promise to be real with emotions. I am ready to bless the world with my presence. The question is, are they ready for this package of joy and laughter? My thought was interrupted like a bowel movement on a missions trip (look for that story later), I flew out and landed on the cold hard floor. This was my first opportunity to forgive man. With a dented head, right then and there, I chose to laugh, forgive, and live life to the fullest. Situations for the rest of my life could be perceived in a positive or negative light and it was all up to me. I have a whole life ahead of me, what am I going to do with it? We will see.

THE PARABLE OF THE SOWER

"A farmer went out to sow his seed. As he was scattering the seed, some fell along the path; it was trampled on, and the birds ate it up. Some fell on rocky ground, and when it came up, the plants withered because they had no moisture. Other seed fell among thorns, which grew up with it and choked the plants. Still other seed fell on good soil. It came up and yielded a crop, a hundred times more than was sown." When he said this, he called out, "Whoever has ears to hear, let them hear." His disciples asked him what this parable meant. He said, "The knowledge of the secrets of the kingdom of God has been given to you, but to others I speak in parables, so that, " 'though seeing, they may not see; though hearing, they may not understand.' "This is the meaning of the parable: The seed is the word of God. Those along the path are the ones who hear, and then the devil comes and takes away the word from their hearts, so that they may not believe and be saved. Those on the rocky ground are the ones who receive the word with joy when they hear it, but they have no root. They believe for a while, but in the time of testing they fall away. The seed that fell among thorns stands for those who hear, but as they go on their way they are choked by life's worries, riches and pleasures, and they do not mature. But the seed on good soil stands for those with a noble and good heart, who hear the word, retain it, and by persevering produce a crop. Luke 8:4-15 NIV

It's very interesting to read this because there are definite times of questioning, "God are we hearing you? I want to see movement or else I'm out." For my personal dream, God, has consistently kept about ten people's hearts interested. I have no doubt that He created my dream (your biggest one you can't do without him) that way so that I wouldn't have it snatched away (the road). For some background, I know I'm called to run a ranch and create growth and forward movement for anyone that wants to come and seek that. I know I cannot do this alone, nor will I. We could have quit with the troubles that have come up for seven years (gravel), or kept worrying about tomorrow, making money and having fun and losing focus (the thorns). We do feel like we have been in the "good ground" on this one. Not that we've arrived, but thank God we didn't miss another dream that God has placed in our hearts only to be quickly snatched up. Thank you Lord for giving us the group of people that keep our feet on the ground, our patience in check, and our hearts searching for the next move. We are "sticking with it until there is a harvest." The only way to do that, in my opinion, is to have a group of people that are seeking His will in what they have "truly heard" concerning the ranch (my dream place in my heart by God). This group has moved me forward in my relationship by leaps and bounds, especially on the questioning days.

Where are you at with your "big dream?" Are you the seed that got something really special, got home and it was immediately snatched up by naysayers or the people that have duct taped you into a small box? Are you the seed that had tons of excitement but didn't invite God in for his leading (the roots weren't deep) and the moment there was a bump or resistance you were done? Are you the seed in the thorns & weeds? Is your dream so choked out by the opinions of others, the worries of tomorrow, unbelief, making riches, or just enjoying the pleasures of life? With a noble and good heart I encourage you to keep going, growing and bear fruit in that dream with patience.

What a great place to be. You have no idea how to complete the task, and you are resting in Him, moving when He tells you to move. It is about the journey and it is about His name being glorified when it comes to pass, not yours.

I encourage you to dive into the good soil, take a look at your inner circle (friends that surround you), and get a group together that will link arms on your dream. Do you truly feel like you were created to do just what you are doing now? Are you questioning if you even know God or have ever had a dream? These are some great questions to ponder for awhile, and I get chills thinking about God revealing that to you. Don't be afraid of sitting in silence until you hear him speak.

Action • Growth • Awareness

1. Listen to Graham Cooke's "Nature of God" Part 1 & 2.

2. Journal about your dreams & answer the questions in this story?

3. Has the word of God fallen in good soil for you?

4. What are some things you know God has asked you to do?

5. What actions can you take to get back in integrity with what you have heard?

6. Whose dreams have you judged and killed off with your thoughts and opinions?

Amazing relationships challenge you to be the best you, link arms with your dreams, cheer with successes, help you find positives in failures and just love you in the moment, especially those moments you can't stand yourself. – Amanda

Judging a person does NOT define who they are, it defines who YOU are. - Unknown

Journal

Insight • Answers • Downloads
AHA's • Wisdom • Findings

CHRISTIAN COLLEGE PRANKS

In college, I loved hanging out with Pete, who was my best friend. My humor was quite unrefined and vulgar, but honestly I was meeting God at the same time period in my life. I found when I choose Him, my old flesh always rose up double time as if fighting for its life. Oh and the need to be liked as well. God had a different plan for me with humor, I just didn't know it yet. In the meantime, the value of vulgar and shock in a Christian college created my muse for four years. This man-boy Pete, was an incredible friend to me, he walked me through my mom's divorce that happened my senior year of high school, the death of my step brother, and many other challenges during college. We didn't have Facebook or even email at that time so we had to be creative with our humor and boy were we. There are a couple of "doozies" that I would like to share with you. Feel free to use them, they aren't copyrighted.

IT ALL STARTED WITH SURPRISE BROWNIES

When you really care about someone you want to thank them with a good ole batch of warm brownies. When you love to harass that someone, you wrap the brownies in a huge pair of women's underwear and mail them through the school post office. I also sent him a toothbrush of a naked woman so he could keep his teeth cavity free. I knew he would love it because using a toothbrush like that at a "Christian" college would be an awesome responses worth the $3 investment. A couple weeks later I sent him the picture below. The laugh we had when Pete called me saying he was really enjoying the brownies and toothbrush was priceless. See, Pete never let me get one over on him, he would always be unmoved and work on his next trump.

HIS TRUMP - BIKING LESSONS

So in college, people made up posters advertising their events. At least that was how it was in the 90's. Pete and I were in computer graphics class and the project was to create a poster advertising an event. I loved mountain biking so I created a poster that advertised how I was going to give mountain biking lessons. I added humor and sass cause it was a "fake" project to be turned in to my teacher only. Full of double entendres like: this will be the ride of your life and I'll work you out till all your muscles get their max performance. Of course, this was to make Pete and I laugh but also push my "straight laced" teacher over the edge. I never got in trouble with teachers with my humor, but walked a very, very thin line. I always knew how far I could go and was thrilled when the teacher would laugh out loud when they didn't want to. I quickly put my name and number on the poster and gave it to Pete to hand in as I was late for my next class.

When I got out of class, about an hour later, to my utter surprise, hundreds of my posters were hanging everywhere at my Christian school. I laughed so hard as I walked through the campus, while every guy that passed by me asked me my prices and what kind of outfit and accessories they should wear. When I got back to my room I had 25 voice mails from different guys leaving incredibly inappropriate messages. Sister, you had better have a back bone if you are going to mess with men and jokes.

MY DOUBLE TRUMP - INTRAMURALS

Intramurals, in my college were highly competitive between dormitory floors. It was our way of getting the sorority and bonding that we desired without the debauchery and drunkenness. We took it seriously and in my junior year, my floor, Alpha Omega won. It was the epitome of team spirit and lead to absolute trash talk between teams.

One day, my roommate Jen, who worked in the intramurals sports office, was helping to clean up the field after a flag football game. Jen, noticed that Youngblood, Pete's floor, had left their prized sack of jerseys on the field. Probably because they were so busy bragging about their win. Now if you know men and their attachment to things like jerseys and sports, then you know this was a super dangerous and scary move for Jen. She quickly grabbed the bag and stuffed it in her stuff. Pete was telling me about the loss later that day and wondering if I heard anything. He also stated how incredibly mad the guys were. This scared me and I kept my mouth shut. It was so bad, that I didn't tell Pete about it until 10 years after college. Silent trump.

We took a bunch of pictures in the jerseys (mildly inappropriate) and then mixed up some pudding and took a picture with them all in the toilet with chunks specifically placed. Then Jen took them back to the office and they were returned to the man-boys making her a "hero" for "finding" the very missed jerseys. Weeks later, through the mail, we sent the headless pictures and toilet shots. The best was to hear Pete tell me about all of this as if I didn't know. He was still very angry and I still had no desire to have a good laugh with him. Silently, I knew I had finally trumped him big time. I was satisfied.

This game went on for four wonderful years. College was a blast because I chose to have an amazing time and laugh a lot. Love you Pete and Young Blood and I hold all of our laughs in my memory bank. Alpha Omega did many other pranks to other floors but my favorite to date was putting fish bait in the ceiling tiles of Red's floor. It was so foul that we could smell it in the elevator days later. I don't think we owned up to that one either. Have I grown up since then? Yes and No. I do not start something that I don't want back even worse. I do however always look for the humor in things and it serves me greatly.

Recently I caught up on the phone with Pete and I told him about the book. He reminded me that the worst I did was write a secret admirer letter with my roommate that was laced with perversion and deeply expressed love. I sent it to over 100 guys through the campus mail. Pete said he was excited himself until he heard and saw other guys bragging about their letter to their friends. How could I forget that one? You tend to forget the evil harsh un-loving things you do. : (

SOMETHING TO PONDER

Here is the thing about life, are you enjoying it and creating fun with your family and friends? Are you laughing more than once a week? If you think back to childhood or school/college/work memories, do you have amazing ones or mediocre? Take a look at why that is. Are you willing to choose in to something different in order to have more fun? Are you so disabled about how you look or caring what people think that you are unwilling to have fun? This could be a huge find for you. Listen, I'm challenging you on this because it has served me for many years. The years of laughter was lacking were the hardest years of my life because I was alone. No one wanted to be around "Debbie Downer." Some people want to know you deeply and from a fun and personal proactive responsible way. This is my trial and this is why its funny and this is what I'm doing to move out of it. Maybe it is time to make a batch of brownies and bring some joy in yours and someone else's life. Who deserves a hot batch of nutty brownies served and wrapped up tight with love in a size 52 pair of mens underwear? By the way, Pete sent me a batch of those two years after graduation and I laughed and cried remembering how much fun we had in our friendship. Love you Pete.

IT'S YOUR LIFE
TO WEED OR NOT TO WEED, THAT IS THE QUESTION?
My most popular blog because of the title only.

I have let my beautiful garden go these last few years because I chose for it to be too hard, overwhelming, not fun, and lonely. I chose to not take care of something that is enriching, and a blessing to myself and others. Do you find that you do that in life? The garden analogy is YOU and the creation is what you want to create with YOU. I have so many people in my life right now that are right along side me. Their gardens are full of weeds, choking out beauty, & in rocky, hard soil. There is one flower in a sea of death. Well, the book of the past is written right? The rest of the book is in yours and Gods hands to create. Weed out that Garden, death, addictions, fears, negative friends & lack of relationship with God in order for Him to bring forth beauty out of that new rich soil.

I finally motivated myself to weed my garden 20 hrs over a couple days. That is crazy, if I had just cared enough to maintain it during the growing process, it would be a quick run through to pluck those "nasty invaders" and keep my garden beautiful. Since reading _The Shack_, I have been journeying with the garden analogy and what God had for me.

God sees us exactly as we are, weeds and all. He sees beauty even when I allow massive sin into my life. The end result of that sin is that it starts to overtake us and choke out the beauty in our lives. As I was weeding, I was in tears that God gives us choices to weed daily, monthly or yearly. The good soil is going to bring all of the good fruit He has imparted in us to share on a daily basis. I was in awe that parts of the garden were completely rock hard dirt, and thorns and of course the weeds flourish there too.

In the last four years, I have chosen to work on myself with God to identify and pluck some of those weeds. This included Personal Development courses, Bible Studies, writing, group prayer sessions, counsel and lastly ACCOUNTABILITY. It has truly been painful, exciting, loving and extraordinary all at the same time. I have accountability in all areas of my life; in personal, business, and spiritual. It is the mulch over lay on the garden in a sense. It keeps a lot of the weeds from coming through, killing most of them. It also allows me to see quickly when a stray weed comes up, so I can easily "pluck" it. Daily maintenance at this point compared to 20 hrs a season is looking really good to me now.

Later as I pruned the tree, I noticed that the new life was coming from an old branch, not the trunk, the main source. I found that to be odd. Why would it try and grow off an old branch? So where in life does that show up? When I choose not to prune and live my own life, the only new life that comes from me is from OLD ways. That is a gross thought. I choose to prune and have accountability. Thank you to those of you that have been my shears, it has helped me move forward quickly into my dreams without fear or caution. Weeding will always be there for all of us. The question is how much of the garden do you want God to use? 25%, 50% or 100%. You choose, you write the end of your book. Look at what is sitting on my pile of weeds, one of my cherished possessions. Thank God, he hasn't been choked out by my lack of weeding. Thank you God for that grace and time.

Action · Growth · Awareness

1. Buy *The Shack* by William P. Young and read as soon as you can.

2. Write Down 10 weeds in your life that are choking you out?

3. Take an honest look at your life, would it serve you to weed anyone out?

Journal

Insight • Answers • Downloads
AHA's • Wisdom • Findings

SMALL **TALL** *tales*

A SONG ABOUT TURNING 40 - COUGARDOM

On the first day of my 40th it kindly gave to me

12 chin rolls
11 cougar outfits
10 grey hairs
9 blurry visions
8 inches of Fupa
7 kegels kegeling
6 smallish brown spots
4 parts a sagging
3 weird growths
2 knees a aching
and a needed makeover for all to see

I HAVE A DREAM TO HELP

A movie that rocked me to the core, was *The Help*. I love truth, I love to express it, bring humor around it, expose it and yet still I find that I have huge places inside me that hide it. Some people don't understand or get "my humor" and sometimes have given me feedback that I am too heavy, too much, and "flee for the hills." Some embrace it and hear my heart. They can dive into the "deep end" and journey through life with me, and some chose out. I'm so thankful for my deep end friends cause it fuels me to keep going. Being understood or "seen" is important to all of us.

I absolutely related to Skeeter the main character and narrator in the movie. Everything about her was somewhat of a mirror image: from not wanting to dress to impress a man, to the crazy curly hair. I believe if I was in that era, I would have been in the kitchen learning about the hearts of the mistreated. I would be the one truly embarrassed of my parents and the white man dishonoring "the help." I believe I would have wanted "the help" to know white people didn't all feel that way nor wanted to follow their family's awful examples of how to treat a human. I have been that way my whole life. I do hope that I will be a voice for others suffering prejudices and exclusion from society. At the minimum I hope that I keep my self in line and pass this down to my boys. When will this be over? Probably in heaven.

There is a line in the movie where Skeeter asks the maid if she ever had a dream. Of course she did! The strength just wasn't there to help her fulfill it before Skeeter stepped in. I honestly wouldn't have the energy or the know how if people hadn't stepped into my dream with me. Is it fulfilled? NO! Am I gonna keep walking forward and watch the unknown unfold before me? YES, but only with God's strength, patience and others support.

A book that blew me away around grace and dreams is True Faced. It is overwhelming on what it spoke to me, I highly recommend it if you are stuck in your dream and are considering on giving up.

"Ever since we were children we have had dreams and hopes of destiny. Some of these dreams are our own, but others came from the very heart of God --and God's dreams never go off the radar screen. Even time, failure or heartbreak can't make us forget them entirely. Still, most of us have tried to stuff them into the attic. We have been rudely awakened out of too many of them, too many times, and each time we lost more and more of the dream. Yet, even if we've forgotten the fiber of these dreams, GOD HAS NOT."

"God's dreams for you are ultimately NOT really about you. Oh, don't misunderstand. They'll bring you some of the best days of your life; you will be fulfilled beyond any imaginable expectations. But God's dreams take form only when they are about others, for the benefit of others. Loving them. Guiding them. Serving them. Influencing them. Filling their heads with dreams and hope. There are no other types of God dreams. Everything else will always, ultimately, taste chalky or dry. God's destiny for you will never be so trivial as building a kingdom for you to enhance

your acclaim. The dream he has prepared custom for you is explosively beautiful and alive. This stunning dream always involves others. Others being freed, healed, convinced of who they really are, convinced that they can fly, convinced His dreams in them can come true."

That is enough to chew on for a week or a lifetime really. So, when I feel fulfilled I am stepping into other's souls with a shovel and helping dislodge the deathly disbelief. Allowing God to work through me to support people into understanding HIM, even when I don't understand HIM myself. Is it what I've always dreamt of? That is still to come but yes, I have shoveled a bunch out of my own life and others have journeyed with me and for that I am truly thankful as that is contentment for me.

"God dearly longs for the day when he gets to hand you that ticket, smile and whisper into your ear, "You have no idea how long I've waited to hand this to you. Have a blast! I've already seen what you get to do. It's better than you could have dreamed. Now hurry up and get on that train. A whole lot of folks are waiting for you to walk into your destiny and into THEIR LIVES."

I believe in you and mostly I believe in ME. Thank you for journeying with me. "You is smart, you is kind and you is important." – The Help

All quotes from--True Faced by Bill Thrall, Bruce McNicol, & John S. Lynch

1. What are your God dreams?

2. Buy and Read at some point <u>True Faced</u> by *Bill Thrall, Bruce McNicol, & John S. Lynch*

3. Watch the movie <u>The Help</u>

4. Listen to the song – <u>Living Proof</u> by Mary J. Blige

Journal
Insight • Answers • Downloads
AHA's • Wisdom • Findings

SMALL **TALL** tales

RUINER OF SERIOUS CHI

"Ssshhh!" I was waiting with my earphones in, for my FIRST yoga class to start. I turn my head to look at the overly righteous woman and obviously serious "yogi" shhhhhhusher. Spit flies from a grey toothed frown onto my cheek and glasses. She takes her patchouli oiled pointer finger and runs it down my lips from my nose to my chin. "Don't be a Chi ruiner." I pull my headphones out of my ears that are pounding out my favorite Snoop Dogg song. "I'm sorry, what?" "This is a room fragranced with the inner child essence and you are ruining my Chi." My eyebrows pucker up to two up-side-down V's and I start doing my exhaling as if I'm in birthing classes. I breathe in deep and choke on the stench that reminds me of my boys first bowel movement. I say back to her "Is that meconium." I think to myself, Oh this is why I haven't been here before. At this point, judgment is out, and I am in a full sarcastic experience of mockery in my head, and easily seen in my body language and facial expressions.

I catch eyes with Terra, and with a look, say it all to each other in a semi smile of sarcasm. Silence at this point would not be attainable. I scan the room and there are spandex that are stretched to their maximum capacity creating more camel toes than in an Egyptian zoo. As I look at the teacher in the "downward dog" position, I get a full view of a participant directly in front of me with short shorts on. I'm thinking this would make my gynecologist blush. Labia much? The sound of the bongo drums beating pulls me back into my focus and positioning of my tailbone arc in the air. The breathing gets well….it gets a little heavy if you know what I mean. Actually, do you know what I mean? I was looking around wondering if someone was in labor, being delivered from a demon or actually making a baby in the front of the room. I finally realize it was just Rita really trying to do "sleeping yogi" and struggling to get her feet out from under her head.

I scan the back mirror, catching my own reflection holding my very un-flexible leg up in the air. I notice and feel that my loose shirt has made its way past my old, tired, off color bra. My fupa (fat upper pelvis area) has displayed its glory to everyone that might happen to be facing that way. In my case that is the entire back row. My clarity on the "why" of the tight outfit quickly educates me. My spandex have sausaged my fat roll up and over my waist band. I am now flushed and expelling large amounts of sweat and we just started the class ten minutes ago.

Next, I figure out how to get into the "happy baby" pose, look over at Terra and she mouths the words "pussssh." I start laughing without sound so hard that tears roll down into my ears and all the muscles in my stomach seize. We both could not pull it together. I took a deep breath, get into downward dog again and suddenly the teacher is a fingernail distance from my backside. The scene from Couples Retreat runs through my head and I clench my butt cheeks together. Boom! Boom! She runs her hand all the way down to my head bending forward and laying on top of my back.

17

I am at a loss for words because I am in a horrific silence. This is a first as well. I have finally been served everything I have ever handed out to people in my life in the shock arena. That's what I call a trump. Namaste this, <u>Happy Gillmore</u> glue eating teacher. Don't touch where my full body suit up to the neck covers. I finally got to lay there and ponder the music and what just happened when the teacher walks by and sprays over our faces whispering "this is tranquility." While grimacing, I can't believe my face was just sprayed with what smells like goat urine. Will I go back for more of that action? Uh yeah, that was awesomely the most uncomfortable I have been in years. Yoga teacher 3, me 0. I sat there in silence and wondered "what would Jesus do?"

#raisingcomedians

At a young age I had freckles and got made fun of by the boy I liked which was devastating at the time. In fact, he took a pen and connected them on my arm. Corbyn, at a young age asked me where freckles came from. I didn't want him to go through my childhood trauma so I told him "they are kisses from God and they are reminders of how much he loves you." He breaks out in laughter, pulls his pants down and bends over. "So you're saying God kissed my butt?"

This morning I made a failed attempt to explain to my boys why it was ok to call a hotdog dog a wiener. All sorts of laughter from the back seat. "Well, can I call a short hairy guy with a long torso a wiener?"

Me: "only if he's barking."
It's a good thing they have a teacher, no home school for me.

One way pictures should not be used to teach would be where a baby comes from. This in fact is better as a verbal description.

Interesting fact and I know this will ruin some of your stories you've told since you were a kid. Baby Ruth's in fact do NOT float in a pool. I love that Tyler was an excited participant in creating the cover of my book.

Proud mom moment - while I am eating corn on da cob Ty yells out in perfect Nacho Libre voice "get that corn outta ma face." We all laughed for a straight 5 minutes. Haven't seen that movie in over a year.

LEANING ON MY OWN UNDERSTANDING = DEATH

Trust in the LORD with all your heart and lean not on your own understanding; in all your ways submit to Him, and He will make your paths straight. Do not be wise in your own eyes; fear the LORD and shun evil. This will bring health to your body and nourishment to your bones. – Proverbs 3:5-8 NIV Bible

Are you in the midst of a downward spiral? Is there confusion, fear, lack of trust, and the need to prove yourself worthy? What do you suppose that is? My take is that is a RED flag that I am leaning on my own ideas and limitations. I recently got "dragged down a path" to a situation that I feel the enemy orchestrated. One of my old-school big lies is that "it isn't worth stepping into peoples lives because you will always get burned." Well that is interesting since I feel called to open up a ranch and facilitate the left behind youth to healing and forward growth. That is precisely why bringing the lies to the light can give you great weapons against darkness. I have stepped in many lives unconditionally (sometimes successfully and sometimes not) and that just plain ticks off the enemy. Notice it and don't let the enemy stop forward growth with you or the people you are involved with. Also allow God to direct your path.

When you are in a battle and blindsided, in my opinion, you have given up your control and let the enemy "ping pong" you around. He is giggling with laughter at how easy it is to push your buttons and take you out of the game for the day, week or month. You see, the people involved, including me, are not the enemy. The enemy could possibly use us to lure each other off the path to wholeness. Where have you, in relationship, been taken off the path of wholeness? Where have you stopped in your tracks and given in to distrust, sin, back-biting, hatred, and protection of your character?

When this happens, I choose awareness and boundaries. Well actually that really means I choose bars or walls to put up that no one will get through. I will not be hurt again. That is exactly Satan's plan. When swirling out of control happens you have to ask for support, get with God and get wisdom and clarity. Your worth doesn't depend on other opinions of you. It seems to me that in our culture people measure their worth and happiness based on a variety of things such as their relationships, intelligence, achievements at school or work, or how much money we make. Interesting, don't you think? Our worth comes from all these things which are the very areas where Satan attacks and steals from us. Hmm just a thought.

"How we handle situations that are beyond our control illustrates whether we are operating with pride and self-sufficiency or with humility and dependence on God." "If we are willing to humbly depend on God and recognize our inability to handle things on our own strength, we will see the power of God bring great changes in our lives." NIV Bible discussion So lean NOT on my own understanding of any situation. Live in Freedom

Action · Growth · Awareness

1. Listen to <u>Refuge</u> by Darrell Evans

2. Can you think of a time you leaned on your own understanding? What was the outcome?

3. Journal about where in life you have confusion.

4. What walls have you put up that no one can get through? Why?

5. Where have you, in relationship, been taken off the path of wholeness? Where have you stopped in your tracks and given in to distrust, sin, back-biting, hatred, and protection of your character?

HEAVY, DEEP AND REAL FUNNY

Journal
Insight • Answers • Downloads
AHA's • Wisdom • Findings

AMANDA SHARP

Journal
Insight • Answers • Downloads
AHA's • Wisdom • Findings

I WAS "THAT GUY" ON THE PLANE

So as a photographer, I have many gigs that take me to other states to shoot for personal development courses. I love the gig and also get to hang with some of my favorite friends all year. On the way home from one of these amazing weekends, I traveled with a friend that also lived in Colorado Springs. His humor was in tune with mine, so once again, it became a scenario of trumping competitions. This one included speaking loudly to each other on a crowded plane. When you play that game, you make sure to mention the most embarrassing conversation you can in order to make points of how many people laugh around you. I had some stiff competition for sure and I believe I won with "so Sheldon did that ointment help that rash I saw you had in the hot tub the other night?" "I wonder if anyone else picked that up from you, I'll have to keep my ears open." You know that kind of laughter way past inappropriate church laughter? You know when you are literally making no noise and you can't find a pause for air. Your face flushes and tears roll out because literally, if you don't have the talent to get the next breath in, you could very well die.

We boarded without seat assignments onto the plane. We sat with a seat between us and kept talking loudly as we were hoping to discourage the third person from sitting there. Selfish? Aren't we all? We were still laughing between comments, we were in physical pain. I took a puke bag for the last passengers getting on and started fake heaving into the paper sack. Loudly, I hoarked into this bag and Sheldon took pictures to post on Facebook. As I was acting to the best of my abilities, I looked up and this lady was staring at me with a smile. She said "Honey, I'm a flight attendant, I've seen it all, now are you going to scoot over?" Busted! We kept going till we landed in Denver because we had a volunteer captive audience and we didn't want to let her down. She told us she had seen it all and we weren't going to disappoint.

Where in your life could you use a laugh that feels like 200 crunches? Play this game in a crowd and practice "being fun." If it isn't natural to you, use some of my lines mentioned above in a crowded place and have a laugh with a great friend or family member. It seriously makes a lot of your worries go away. I will do this with my sons when they get older because I have been priming them for this.

MAKES ME WANT TO STOMP

Okay, breathe deep cause this is going to have some energy with it. I just came across a song that is one of my favorites in high school. <u>Stomp</u> by Kirk Franklin. Since I love to dance, you can imagine how I responded in High School when I went to a church with this kind of Praise and Worship. I haven't felt God in that way, that really special, jazzed way, in awhile. If you'll do me the honor, turn up your volume, walk away from this book, find this song on youtube.com and I will dance and laugh with you until your belly hurts and your soul fills! Play it until you are in an out of body, surrendered experience.

My boys and I have laughed and danced so hard to this song before, and it was awesome. The first time I did that, I visualized a stream of people in my life and how much we laugh together when we are being crazy and unreserved. If you didn't even tap a toe you might want to get checked out. If you have such a huge "looking good program" that you couldn't dance to a 90's song, then you missed out. DEBBIE DOWNER, TRY AGAIN. Seriously don't continue reading until you experienced something new for yourself. I get it, I felt stupid as well. What do you bring to a concert of a band that makes you wildly crazy? Step in to that.

I laughed so hard in joy that it brought tears to my eyes. My experience was as if something VERY heavy broke off of me. It felt great and I wanted more. Talk about setting some context for the day. What is that? What broke off and released when I was surrendered to the experience?

You have to know this didn't just happen during the song. I had been praying and asking God as to why I was so discontent, had sadness and heaviness most of my life. I really found immediate results when I gave up the need to be liked. I've practiced this for awhile now and thus far, on a very deep level, it has changed my whole outlook. I've heard that it's none of my business what others think of me. This to me is a Fear of Loss, meaning you don't want to lose friendships if you do something they don't approve of.

I have watered the fear of loss seed since childhood. In many ways, I've recreated LOSS for myself over and over. I know my dad choosing out of relationship with me at a very young age greatly affected me. Since then, I've pretty much attracted it to myself in different relationships. On a deep level I came across the realization and truth that I keep recreating this so I can prove myself right; that I'm not worth fighting for and people will leave me if I do something they don't approve of. This creates a life of people pleasing in my opinion.

Thought I'd give you a moment with that thought cause it's a deep seeded TRUTH.

I was in my FEAR hardcore, feeling like "no matter what I do, I will LOSE people." I prayed and fell asleep asking for help. Sometime in my slumber, I heard very clearly, "how easily are you going to give your heart away?" I knew immediately that the root was pulled out, cause something clicked in my thought process. This didn't mean I will never have a fear of loss again and now I'm aware of when I'm reserved because I don't want to lose someone or have the need to please them. Sometimes when you have a fear of LOSS, you bring people in close and then smother them, control, manipulate, or emotionally tether them to you. It gives a fake sense of worth, feeling good and happy for a short time. What it really does to me internally is make me crazy emotionally. It is an endless pit and void to fill, always ending in unmet expectations, loneliness and more loss and rejection.

I have since walked in the freedom that I have amazing relationships and I don't have to manage and upkeep them to pristine state with no flaws. I get to be joyful because I'm not exhausted. I get to receive abundance in conversations, connections and financially as I walk in the freedom I have asked God to give me. I have to say I feel truly JOYFUL and I don't know that I've ever allowed myself to experience that.

When I have my identity in man it is a complete train wreck. When I have my identity in God, I have an amazing life.

When you find this freedom or any other it might make you want to STOMP.

Action • Growth • Awareness

1. Listen to the song <u>Stomp</u> by Kirk Franklin until you have a massive breakthrough of joy. What did you experience and release off you today? If nothing, stomp some more.

2. Send an email to Amanda at <u>sharpdesignsinc@mac.com</u> and tell her what you are committed to releasing for good. Put in the subject – I stomped this out today.

AMANDA SHARP

Journal
Insight • Answers • Downloads
AHA's • Wisdom • Findings

HAMSTER BURIAL

Status Feed on Facebook: "Who's going to put Dunkin in a box for me?" My boys would like to bury him next to Teddy in the back yard. "Ahhhhhh, I know I wasn't called to this." If I ignore it, their dad can do it on Thursday......discuss. (Possibly 8 days of hanging out in a cage) Please Help!

Here are the choices I gave for what I should do with our newly deceased hamster:

De-friend Amanda on Facebook as now she has crossed a line.

Aerial Burial - fling him down the hill out back after a ceremony of course.

Make a tuxedo & a hat out of paper.

Wait for their dad to do it on Thursday and pretend it happened that morning.

Go get another one and tell them Jesus healed him? (That was my sac religious idea.)

Give him mouth to mouth.

Start acquiring taxidermy skillz and stuff that bad boy.

Add him to your stew, no one will know.

Stuff him and take as a mascot on your next trip for all your pictures.

Sell him on Ebay or Craigslist as slightly used and quiet. Sleeps during the day and night.

Get ripped a new one by my P.E.T.A animal hugging friends and apologize once and only once.

DEDICATION

Let's take a moment to honor Dunkin, our hamster of three years. He fought the fight (literally killed our other one), ran 1000 miles (on that frigging squeaky ass wheel), chewed through numerous wood structures and toilet paper rolls, marked off escaping "this hell hole of a cage" off his dream board. He was a mediocre lover, fantastic biter, and had the best fluffy long hair that waved in the wind of his wheel rocking ass. Bye Dunkin......named lovingly after a turd by Tyler.

MASK OR BARE TODAY?

"Don't be so hard on yourself, I can bring good even out of your mistakes. Your finite mind tends to look backward, longing to undo decisions you have come to regret. This is a waste of time and energy, leading only to frustration. Instead of floundering in the past, release your mistakes to Me. Look to me in trust, anticipating that my infinite creativity can weave both good choices and bad into a lovely design. Because you are human, you will continue to make mistakes. Thinking that you should live an error-free life is symptomatic of pride. Your failures can be a source of blessing, humbling you and giving you empathy for other people in their weaknesses. Best of all, failure highlights your dependence on ME. I am able to bring beauty out of mistakes. Trust Me, and watch to see what I will do." - Jesus Calling

The quote above is powerful. What a great love note from God. If you watch what is swirling around you, there are intricate consistencies, a message of healing if we choose to be healed. Drama and pain possibly, if we don't.

When I have the opportunity to have a "kid free" couple of hours or day, I usually have to be pro-active and not fill it up with things that take me away from God. I heard this time "go to the World Prayer Center and sit in my lap?" The World Prayer Center is a great place that is open 24 hours and has constant live or recorded praise and worship. I was asked out on a date by God and I didn't turn it down. I was surrounded by a full view of the mountain range at sunset! I knew there was something big on the table that we would be chatting about. I chose to take off my mask and be bare, to allow a download of emotions, to release all to Him, to surrender. My jaw tightened as I peeled the mask off my tender skin, my throat clenched knowing a rush of healing tears was coming. It was real, and it was the safest place I knew to be, just ME. Well, safe before God that is.

What do you think about masks? I think we have such a fine collection that we are appalled when we look in the mirror bare faced. It's that foreign of a face to us. If you don't believe me, stare in the mirror ten minutes without looking away. Write down all the self talk that comes up. That ten minutes alone will tell you everything you need to know. My self talk certainly speaks about me even when I'm unaware. It seeps into everything in my life.

This is what I told myself when I looked into the mirror.

"You must hide yourself, find people that allow you to hide the real you, you are too much, you are not to be cherished, you are to be hidden. Find someone that wants to hide you as you aren't that great, after all, they might be embarrassed of you." It flowed out with ease, "Keep bringing humor into others lives, it feels awesome right? Then they won't know, they will see joy right, put on that joker mask girl, it's all you got. People don't like truth seekers, they like laughing. Keep lathering people with praise and soon it will come back, okay not really but you're doing a noble thing. Keep digging girl, isn't digging people out of the grave awesome? I'm sure they'll have time to dig you out when you need it most. Come on really? No one has time for you when you are in the pit, that is draining. Actually run like hell, you're being pulled in. By the way, did you know you are crazy? Oh and if you are real with people, you will suffer loss, do you want more of that, put on that damn mask Amanda, the mime one would be great and then your mouth will be closed. What do you have to say anyways? Nothing you hypocrite." "There is not one subject you have mastered, you are a hypocrite!"

If Jesus glories in us and finds us a rare jewel to show off as his bride, why would we settle for anything else? If Jesus cusses, I'm sure he cusses when he sees us go out and accept the falseness that others AND MOSTLY ourselves project as truth.

Masks bring shame don't they? I have literally been blindsided lately wearing my mask of "I got this" pride in the honor of protecting and helping others and believing I should be hidden. Martyr pride is something else man, you feel good for a time until you realize all that did was literally get rid of a limb. "Pat yourself on the back girl. Oh you cant, you're missing your arm! All for Christ, chin up!"

How stupid am I? I'm not, it's just how did I not see this? Oh because the mask has tiny slits in it. I can only see life through a vague blurry seedy perception. My hot breath creates yet another discomfort and foggy film over my vision.

Do I truly want people to fall in love with me, the real me, or the masked woman? Conforming to please others is ripping everyone off. Based on results, I want you to enjoy the mask and not complain cause the real me unveiled is passionate! Be very clear that I'm right there to help you super glue your masks on your face as well. Sorry it tears your skin when you take it off. My bad.

People pleasing is a brutal form of manipulation. It drips with the enemies plan of binding you in a mask and the facade that goes with it. I think that's why I'm compelled to write in this heart surgery format. I want to be released from emotional imprisonment. I want to nark on the enemies cheap seedy tricks and I want to abolish this form of death in my life. Hopefully it will shine a light on your darkness as well and you can start pulling off the masks.

Ultimately, all will come to the light right? My theory has always been take it up with God privately lest you be found out by hundreds in a media format. Basically, take off your own mask instead of letting the mockers do it for you. Well, this is me taking it up with God. I never want to be blamed for pulling the wool over someone's eyes, I rather bring up a subject that is real to me and let you chose in or out.

Actually this style of writing allows me to be me, bare and at peace with whom He's created. A true original masterpiece. Although I've printed many copies of me to hand out, the original is always there.

"Our background and circumstances may influence who we are, but we are responsible for who we become." - Unknown

Instead of accepting the mask that man holds in his hand, intending for me to play small, let them see the light that shines out of a barren soul girded in HIS love, be me, be mask-less. Playing small doesn't serve anyone, especially me.

I just watched the movie <u>Soul Surfer</u>. A great movie about a girl who is talented in surfing and a shark takes one of her arms. Did she quit? No she became a better surfer than ever. When loss and devastation come, you have a choice don't you? To quit, or to have such immense character built, that you laugh as you look back at the demolished path, truly thankful for the trial. The woman I have become over the years is humbling. Humbling because, I wouldn't trade in my loss, as the relationship built is not easily shaken. I prayed for this! I got my prayers answered.

I'm inspired to be ME! Time to burn the masks that I'm AWARE of and possibly move people out that allow me to sell myself short and hide.

Growth or decay, those are the only choices. The way you invest your love, is the way you invest your life. Invest your love mask-less.

When I originally wrote this, I pondered if I should add it to my book. On the way home there was a car in front of me with the license plate 044-**MSK**. I laughed and added it to the book.

Action • Growth • Awareness

1. Watch the movie Soul Surfer.

2. Buy <u>Jesus Calling</u> by Sarah Young and read it for daily inspiration.

3. Stand in front of the mirror & record every thought you have looking at yourself for ten minutes. That journey alone will give you all the feedback you need.

3. List 50 things that are amazing about you.

HEAVY, DEEP AND REAL FUNNY

Journal

**Insight • Answers • Downloads
AHA's • Wisdom • Findings**

AMANDA SHARP

Journal

Insight • Answers • Downloads
AHA's • Wisdom • Findings

Unleash Your LAUGHTER
FACEBOOK STATUS FEEDS THAT GET A RESPONSE

I believe personally that Facebook was created for me or my personality type. Being a person that views life in quite the odd way, it brings great joy for me to put up a status feed that makes people LOL (Laugh out loud). I go for the shock value and I don't go for giggles. I go for the whole enchilada of shock. I long for the comment that says, "I actually just peed a little too," "I haven't laughed that hard in a year." This isn't about a reputation to be seen as proper and PC, this is about creating joy and laughter in others lives through the mundane things of life. Hope you enjoy some of my best stuff.

My grandpa just loudly predicted that Tyler would be a fat diabetic by 20. Got to love family gatherings. Maybe he means Phat? Old people = awesome.

I'm thankful, sure. I don't have a turkey body, weird webbed feet and a big red googly thing hanging from my chin. I'm thankful I'm not a turkey this week roasting in the oven with crap shoved.......um in my neck. I'm thankful you can't take out my heart and insides as easily as taking out the sack of giblets and tossing it on the counter. Of course I have had a few relationships where I felt like that sack. Haven't we all? I'm thankful I don't have to sit in an oven for 8 hours letting life pass before my eyes and realizing I really didn't have a life.

Just went on a hot date with a sultry, fantastic, funny, gorgeous, amazing person.......me.

Who wants a cyber hug? You get to choose whether it is a Christian side hug, full frontal or just one that people get uncomfortable and question if we are siblings or lovers.

"Mom, I love your beautiful eyes and teeth, even though they have plaque on them and are yellow. Oh, did I just ruin the love that I just gave." –Tyler

Sometimes in my room, I wear stretchy pants. – Nachooooooo (from movie <u>Nacho Libre</u>)

Hey guys, my boy wants to know if he'll be able to do that crab back bend push up when he is older? Please send pictures of you doing it so I can tell him what to look forward to and that yes, yes you can.

Headed to the pool with the kids and not to drop them off either if you know what I mean.

Should I vote?

I was thinking about settling for the guy at the bar who said I was pretty?

Anyone want to argue religion, sports or politics? Oh wait, I just fell asleep on my own question.

REFINERS FIRE – LET THE FECAL MATTER RISE

It has taken me awhile to write this one because my head has been jammed up in a dark place. I do want freedom, I do want release from my flesh, and I do want peace. AND I can't have any of that without God, in my opinion. My experience is God only grants those things when we are in His lap. Crawling out is my choice, and what I create out of His lap and by myself is questionable.

Am I who I want to be? Not even close. I want to be like Jesus and we are all clear I'm not. I want to perfect my response with every situation thrown at me. I want to be kind, loving, accepting and non-judgmental. Why am I still searching for tangible love as if HE is NOT enough? I want to let you in. I want to not be affected by people's actions. I want to turn the other cheek. I want to give grace, and I don't want to be used or be a place people wipe the fecal matter off their shoes. How do **I** get there?

I don't. I am human and so are YOU. My understanding is that we aren't Jesus, and it is specifically set up that way so that we will NEED and request Him in our lives and decisions. He wants to be asked for His help as He is a gentleman. I actually don't regret anything that has occurred in my life because it has been a refiners fire. In that fire, much has risen to the top. My response is the only thing I can take as my true character. I have a choice to sit in the findings of that or have HIM scrape off the refuse and move on. I can choose to be content, that I am not perfect, and when I am squeezed hard enough, something crazy is going to seep out of my pores. I believe that is the grace room. The flip side of this is that I have immense character created from my fires. I am more loving, kind and compassionate than I use to be. I have changed in so many areas and I am teachable, when I choose. When I choose that, I learn five times faster.

I am NOT to be perfect, I am to strive for holiness, as I am who I am by the grace of God.

Do be careful, if you smell smoke and see fire around me, step back as you could be the receiver of devastation. If you set the fire under me, then kindly step away, please stop stirring, and release the need to be right that I should look how you need me to. God is the one that changes me. We are all in our own pots and that is where grace comes in when our worlds collide. I know every person has been in my life for a reason, some to deeply love me and some to create a fire that helps me recognize my impurities. We burn each other and God is the salve when we do. Please do NOT hear that I am okay with us mistreating each other. I am open to forgiveness and moving on. So instead of going into blame and "I'm such an awful person, look what I always create" go into "Lord help me, this is not great what I create and I want to be more like you."

"Character is both developed and revealed by tests, and all of life is a test. You are always being tested. God constantly watches your response to people, problems, success, conflict, illness, disappointment, and even the weather! We don't know all the tests God will give you, but we can predict some of them, based on the Bible. You will be tested

by major changes, delayed promises, impossible problems, unanswered prayers, undeserved criticism, and even senseless tragedies. In my own life I have noticed that God tests my faith through problems, tests my hope by how I handle possessions, and tests my love through people." --The Purpose Driven Life by Rick Warren

I can tell you with the Waldo Canyon fires in Colorado Springs, which demolished our states beauty and many houses, we are seeing what character we have as a community. We are being tested to see what we will do in absolute devastation. It is perceived as devastation because now we are uncomfortable in the huge change made for us, some literally out on the streets. A horrific example that life can change in an instant and an immediate realization of the foundation we are standing on? I wouldn't be alive if mine wasn't in Christ. My previous foundation burnt to the ground and I was standing there naked and embarrassed with what I created. Now, I stand with HIM and WE walk through life together, me striving for more of His qualities and Him giving me grace when I royally fail (in my eyes, not His).

"Every day is an important day, and every second is a growth opportunity to deepen your character, to demonstrate love, or to depend on God. Some tests seem overwhelming, while others you don't even notice. But all of them have eternal implications. The good news is God wants you to pass the tests of life, so he never allows the tests you face to be greater than the grace he give you to handle them. The Bible says God keeps his promise, and he will not allow you to be tested beyond your power to remain firm; at the time you are put to the test, he will give you the strength to endure it, and so provide you with a way out. The most important test is how do you act when you can't feel Gods presence in your life. What do you do when your character is being tested as God draws back?" --The Purpose Driven Life

As I have been in thought around this blog, my son, who has a close connection to the spirit brought me this note. I definitely take this love note from my son and it warms my heart and I know in the back of my head he is a messenger from God

Action • Growth • Awareness

1. Listen to <u>It's your life</u> by Switchfoot

2. Listen to <u>By your side</u> by 10th Ave. North

3. Buy and read at some point <u>Purpose Driven Life</u> by Rick Warren

4. What tests have you had in your life and what was your initial response to them.

5. Are you striving for perfection? How is that serving you?

HEAVY, DEEP AND REAL FUNNY

Journal
Insight • Answers • Downloads
AHA's • Wisdom • Findings

AMANDA SHARP

Journal

Insight • Answers • Downloads
AHA's • Wisdom • Findings

SMALL **TALL** tales

MOSES AND THE BURNING BUSH

Well, well, here we are. This little story truly has brought so much laughter from my friends. It is side splitting, hold in your sphincter kind of story if you can get past judgment. Actually, if you are a "judger" for a living, or easily offended when Bible stories are used out of context, you should stop right here. This is to protect my Grandma. She doesn't need to be judged, she's in her nineties. This woman is southern to the core including the love of everything shrimp. She is six foot and loves life to the fullest. She is one of the greatest women of faith I know and was a tirelessly awesome wife to my late Grandfather of sixty five years.

Here is the deal, she is one of the funniest women I know and she also deeply loves God. So, what do you do with that? Do you act like two different people and change around the audience? I believe now, a little of both. You "read a room" and decide what you can bring to the room to create a space where people experience joy, love and acceptance. Laughter, in my experience has opened up some of the most healing conversations, and connected relationship. Laughter in my family has created amazing relationships between the women; we can laugh and cry in the same story and even go to God. It is heavy, it is deep, it is real and it is so funny.

Sometimes, if not most, you can let your serious side take a break and laugh at what is on your plate. Quite frankly, sometimes we are chewing on a rump roast and it's time to laugh and go out for Chinese. Step back and start creating the space with the people around you that want in desperately and don't know how to get there with you. If you are extremely controlling, abrasive and hard to converse with, you will always get to be right that you aren't worth knowing or being close to. Your fun side is the most powerful side in my opinion. Why? Because it allows people in.

"Insecurity thrives in a predictable environment....if you'd like to change that, hang out with someone that is unpredictable and fun. Having to "look good" all the time manifests insecurity in unpredictable situations." -Amanda

Back to Moses and my point. I was home from college for the summer and my Gma was there. She is a fan of the polyester underwear and mu'u mu'us with hideous designs. It's like a tent with a zipper from knees to neck. So I'm hanging out with her in the kitchen where she is sweating it out over the stove and I happened to catch her scratching in her special place. I smile and let it go. Again, this happened. I finally said "Gma you got a little itch there?" She turned around, raised her eyebrows and gave me her serious animated grimace. "Honey child, I wouldn't wish this on my worst enemy." "What's going on Gma? Do you want me to pray or lay hands on you?" I laugh and say in witty twang. She continues in all seriousness. "This my friend, gives a whole new meaning to Moses and the burning bush." First time in a while I didn't have anything to say. "Well, have you washed your bath tub lately?" "Have you been wearing the same pair of underwear for a week?"

After the shock wore off I began to realize that my humor is a generational and learned behavioral response to all situations. I am proud of this being passed down. That story has been told to many people and gotten the same response. Here's the thing, you can't tell her I told you. She feels it would ruin her witness as an amazing follower of Christ. In my opinion, humor opens people up to get "real" about their lives and be vulnerable. I have found this to be true and that is why I am writing this book this way. Live in the now. Enjoy life. There is so much funny going on all around you. Take a moment to look at the "ailments or irritations" going on in your life. Laugh out Loud. If you aren't laughing you are probably a total drag to be around. Life is not that serious and there is always a humorous slant to all situations that come your way. Hey, its just a suggestion that has been an amazing tool for me. If you struggle with this, hang out with funny people. This does not mean you need to be funny at all. Just enjoy the "different take" on the subject, take deep breaths and realize it's okay to not have a hard ass, offended response to everything.

Unleash Your LAUGHTER

Create a dance party at your house. Start small and "Napoleon Dynamite" that bad boy all by yourself. Work it big time and really give it your all. Don't stop until you have completely released the fear of what you look like. Who cares? The best dancer in the room is the one that doesn't care. What goes with that is the most joyous, magnetic, laugher that can affect a whole crowd. I know this from many events. Next, enroll your family in a dance party until everyone is laughing through the songs. Your next gig will be a room full of un-expecting people, turn on the music and stay committed until you have enrolled the whole group. I am up to a room of 50 people but haven't gotten 100% of the room enrolled but a mosh pit of screaming jumping adults is fantastic. When you have done that, walk the streets where music would be and enroll a stranger in breaking it down with you. I did this in San Francisco one time and I almost started crying because of the joy I had and created and gave with the older man. It released everything I was thinking about. Life stopped and I was filled up and overflowing. It is such a blast and the biggest thing you conquer is your need to look good. This builds self confidence in an unbelievable way. Please email or Facebook me your whole story, I can't wait to hear it. sharpdesignsinc@mac.com

So I tried to do the new sexy penciled in eyebrows I see online. What do you think?

WEATHERING THE STORM.....ON THE JOURNEY

Who would have thought that country music would be filling up my heart with great captures of life and the journey. The quotes throughout are words that God has given me in the last month to keep me going, I hope they fill you up as well. You can go to the action steps now or after reading this.

This subject has been brewing in me for a couple months. It is raw, vulnerable, sliced to the core and yet, this is our journey to HIS legacy. I do want you to know I only write if I am literally moved to and I don't mean by my flesh. It is a humbling process. I don't like to talk just to talk. I do get a chill and swirled of fear as I reread some of my writing, but that is soon fleeting. There are a couple reasons I put my stuff out there. One for extreme accountability, stop the enemies plan, and if it supports someone else in the world to move forward, mainly me, then it is worth my time.

I have been in mental torment and anguish over this dream of how to acquire and own a ranch. Moving forward, and literally losing everything along the way. I still see the light at the end of the tunnel though and it truly catapults me forward. I am not who I was even three months ago, I have been stripped down, wounded, beaten and robbed. Not door mat style either, I put up a good fight. I have been literally left to rebuild who I am with only what HE thinks I am. Look into the mirror and what do you see?

"Nor the applause nor the scorn of others should be of any consequence to you." "Complexities are nothing to Me. They exist only in your mind, sown by the enemy to dull your faith." "Leave the Diagnosis & Mechanics to Me." All Quotes from Jesus Calling – Sarah Young

I am on the journey and yes, I am quite clear much had to be stripped from me in order for me to be ready to take on "the dream." It hasn't looked at all what I hoped it would. The blinders are off and baby it's grim what I've built with my own efforts in four decades. The sand construction is being sadly swept by the tide.

"Leave the miracles to Me. You BE and I will DO."

Is HIS calling worth it? Yes it is. Is it embarrassing when we are many years into the process and not quite there? No, actually the journey is worth it all. It scares me to read Bible stories that have long waiting periods. Have I left most of my old self on the path trekked? Yes, and there is still more to go. There are pieces I have run back and reattached with fish line –sure to hold.

"You need only to preserve your souls integrity. This is enough to fully occupy your energies and attention."

I have learned that I am not God, and that when I do play God, I royally mess up. I am learning that He truly loves me and sees me. I am learning that I have to trust and let go. Literally a real life "trust fall." I am learning the only hand you can hold onto is HIS. Is it worth the mocking & the dis-belief around me, sucking the life and joy out of me? Well, I am still growing and moving forward. The pace wouldn't be gold worthy but I'm moving.

"Never cling to any trouble, hoping to resolve it yourself, but turn it over to Me. In doing so, you will free me to work it out."

So without Story, I have literally lost one thing after another, just trust me on that. I have also gained one thing after another. Slow building, but this has got to be on the "solid rock" this time right? Things are literally separating and lining up at lightning speed. There is much loss and much grief looking one way and the other complete miracles and favor. Then one last wake-up call to really drive home the goodness…..

On January 10, 2010 (My deceased Step-Brothers Birthday), I was a part of a near death experience in my car. Driving home in the snow, beautiful day, wheels spun out and threw me into the center of the highway against the wall. I opened my eyes and was facing the oncoming traffic. I watched a van fish tail on the snow packed highway and miss my car. How? There is only one answer for that. – God. I have never experienced that much peace in my life. It was calm, my thoughts were clear and I didn't try to figure it out. I turned my car around in the highway and drove off. I put my hazards on and drove slowly the rest of the way to the next stop. With the wiper fluid gone, I soon had no visibility of the front of my car. I was scared to get off the road b/c I clearly had traction issues. The sun blared into my windshield and I was visually impaired. Well, I'm here to tell this story so the ending was obviously good.

I want to encourage you with this. Although life is literally spinning out of control, hitting me on every side, and visually impairing me, I still choose to grow. I would rather die giving life a valiant effort and hopefully bless one soul, then sit in a box of fear and never make a step forward because I'm afraid to fail. Well friends, failure is inevitable – I have more failures this month then I have had in ten years. My character will grow through perseverance and I will abound in hope, love and faith as I choose LIFE instead of DEATH.

I am blessed beyond belief and am in gratitude for all the things God is doing. Look back at the people that are choosing out and pray for them. Forgive and forgive and forgive, and clutch the hand of the most high and walk with literally the lamp that only lights your feet on your path. He is the light into MY darkness and the breath that I breathe.

"Do NOT be anyone's answer, let them choose & own their choices. You are not their savior, I AM"

Just keep moving from one life choice to the next. You are doing great.

1. Listen to these songs

   <u>Anyway</u> by Martina McBride

   <u>I hope you dance</u> by Ronan Keating

   <u>All I can say</u> by David Crowder

2. What are you going to choose around your circumstances?

3. Can and will you give it back to God?

4. Find Sean Stephenson Dance Party on Youtube.com

AMANDA SHARP

Journal
Insight • Answers • Downloads
AHA's • Wisdom • Findings

SMALL **TALL** tales

FACEBOOK STATUS FEEDS THAT GET A RESPONSE

I'm going to leave the slang and poor grammar because I feel it is a take from my humor.

If Snoop D.O double G could sing praise and worship, my life would be full and perfect.

The flight attendant just said "if you're on the aisle, tuck in your body parts so the drink cart doesn't take one of them off when we go by."

I'm gonna let u guess how long this rabbit's head (Peep candy) has been on my garage step. My original point was to have my boys see how much they drop all over the house, but it has back fired cause I don't see it anymore. I told my boys why it was there. They laughed and stepped over it again. Passive aggressive never works for me, back to dripping sarcasm "Look! the Easter bunny died in our garage kiddos and its body was eaten by rats, save the head, its all he has!"

I'm kinda the person that if ur gonna do it, do it well and all out. Forgot gym socks and swimsuit so this is gonna be a step outta the comfort zone. I don't have a looking good program.

Just saw the trash guy texting and swinging off the back of his truck almost getting hit by a car. Classic. That msg has to be sent now ehh. Another dies-texting story, just not while driving. I guess that's not illegal. LOL

You're the kind of person I would wear a burka backwards for........but mostly for me actually.

I was reminded early this morning why kids are awesome, as I plunged down an elephant size turd again. Nothing like the juices of greatness splashing on your feet as you give it your all. Now off to help Tyler in class which reminds me why birth control is important. The last time I helped, the kiddos asked me to ask Siri something. I mumbled a simple question and Siri responded, "sorry Douche bag (my chosen nick name), I don't understand what you are asking."

My friend's eighty year old mom was caught standing in front of the TV just staring intently with a cocked head. To her surprise it was, SNL's "Dick in a box." "Want an ice-cream sandwich mom?"

Mmmmmm rat tails, haters gonna hate. Actually, everyone is gonna hate.

I made my kids do a dance off before I would cook dinner and harshly judged their moves. Is that wrong? I totally see the counselor siding with me on this one.

A great letter from my son Tyler who is also the one at a family birthday party in the pool by himself with the noodle strategically placed to balance him. Some pictures don't need captions.

WHAT'S REALLY GOING ON ANYWAY?

Great question. I believe God is now giving me the strength to tell you. Let me start by saying that through a deep loss comes every emotion known to man. I have waded through much of these and have chosen a very close inner circle of friends to walk this out with me. After all, if I completely gave into my flesh and raw emotions, there would be a few houses burned down. Instead, my accountability team and ALWAYS God has been there to create a space of TRUE healing. Here is the other catch and snag. How do you share with people where you are at in life and be completely personally responsible for only yourself? Well, I'm praying through this as I write, and with HIS help, I will be eloquent, loving, forgiving, and personally responsible.

So here it is -- my husband and I, after 14 years, are separating and moving toward divorce. This is a choice he feels is necessary for our kids to have a great upbringing. This was created six months ago officially. I have chosen to sit in God's lap with all of my emotions, dread, let down, pride and yes, even be responsible for what I did and didn't create in the relationship. Bottom line, God has given me great healing, peace, gratefulness, understanding, and hope for the future. Can God bring us back together? Absolutely! That is why I haven't wanted to give this story "LEGS" as they say. Does God have another plan? We will see. Thank you to my inner circle for holding my heart in a safe place until I was ready with God to share. Here's the thing, I have absolute peace that God has us in HIS hands and HE will create what He will out of this mess. He also doesn't make us robots and gives us free choice to make decisions with or without Him.

Why don't you air it on Facebook? We all know that answer right? How numb, how hurtful, how low can you go? It is sad to say, but dreading changing my status from married to blank is extremely scary and emotionless. How do you get to have an intimate conversation with all the people I have relationships with? The answer is, you don't. I can see your faces now, over twenty of you, "why didn't she trust me with this information?" I finally chose to NOT choose the road of "I need to "BE RIGHT" and prove to everyone what a victim I am." My intention was NOT to gather up an army that would fight with me to the end. I don't hate him. My intention was to go right to God and crawl in his lap. It was definitely NOT in my plan to seek approval from man because most of the people I run with are Pro-Marriage and figuring it out. I was even told, "You are a Christian, divorce is not an option." Needless to say, a small group of prayer warriors was a better fit for me.

Here's the thing, I have been praying for over a year for God to give me more LOVE in my heart. I am called to do this ranch idea, and severely questioned my ability to LOVE, truly LOVE. They say be careful what you ask for, right? This is true, cause now I'm in a situation to chose, LOVE or HATE. It's taken a couple months but I choose LOVE. I choose to love and respect him and his decision, I choose to Love myself enough to ask for help, I choose to raise incredible, Godly boys that will not experience emotional craziness and pain because we can't behave in front of each other. I wanted to try something different than my usual "go to" flesh response.

Some of you are pulling out the Bull**** card right now. I can hear the sound of the paper slapping up against your forehead. Well, I have to release my need to care what you think about us in this situation. "It's none of my business what people think of me." I love that quote. The other thing I have learned in life is fear of being found out as a fraud, or being judged. If you think about that, the ONLY reason that has any power over you is because of how harshly you judge others. We know deep down that that fear is strong because we know how hateful and unloving we have been around others' mistakes and pain. I could have typed that coming from I, but I didn't.

Let's be really honest here, I have a huge and harsh judgment on divorce and now what? Where do I go from here? Well, I'm choosing to keep on walking through the doors that have NEVER slammed shut. My knuckles aren't bloody in the door I'm trying to keep open. It is just happening, it will be a miracle and God will be acknowledged through this. I'm clear my lame human status did not create any of this.

The ranch is still very much on our hearts and souls. Our board was dumb founded at what is occurring in my life but open to see what the heck God is doing here. Well, my guess is He is making the best out of what we humans tried to create ourselves – a royal mess. The enemy is NOT going to win on this one. I refuse to pack a couple suitcases of victim-ness and lay down in self pity. It just doesn't look good on me. I do know without a doubt that God has me in his hands.

I can only hope that everyone experiences that Love and I know I've only touched on a portion of it. So far, it is amazing, crazy, love. As one of my friends told me on the phone – "Amanda, if you really knew how much Jesus loved you, you would have joy and no fear at all." Wow, that is true. So, since then I have been on a quest for HIS LOVE. Be careful what you ask for because you just might get it. From experience, this LOVE I'm talking about breaks you down, carefully nudges you to rethink your judgment, and asks you to forgive. That my friends, is something you can't grasp unless you are willing to NOT BE RIGHT in ALL situations.

So coming from a place of NOT NEEDING TO BE RIGHT, I am running toward the goal. That goal includes my soul's integrity and kicking negative self talk and stories out. This is a journey to HIS legacy and that means time to die to myself, which is pride. I embrace it without reservation because quite frankly, I have nothing to lose. I hope this encourages one person to get out of the cesspool of pity and choose LIFE today. I know there is DEEP pain all around us. There has been so much loss amongst my close friends in the last year it is devastating. I do know, the ones choosing God are doing well.

There is a fine line of lying to people and saying all is good and protecting your heart as you heal. I hope this finds a safe haven in your heart. I do know that HE has all my boys in HIS hand. I have no control over the outcome but I do have control over what I choose. This is what I choose. HIM.

"I am deeply loved, totally forgiven, fully pleasing, totally accepted, and complete in Christ." --<u>Search for Significance</u> by Robert McGee

Action • Growth • Awareness

1. Listen to <u>Unfailing God</u> by New Life Worship

2. Listen to <u>Amazed</u> by Desperation Band

3. Do you have a great "inner circle" to support you in forward growth or are you surrounded by victims and blamers?

4. Who do you have harsh judgment on? Who do you feel you need to be right with? Can you come to a place of healing and not need to be right that you deserve something from them? I have experienced tremendous forgiveness when I have let go the need to be right or the need to get an apology.

Unleash Your LAUGHTER

Waiting for my adorablazz. To all the girls who are in a hurry to have a boyfriend or get married, a piece of Biblical advice: "Ruth patiently waited for her mate Boaz." While you are waiting on YOUR Boaz, don't settle for any of his relatives: Broke-az, Lyin-az, Cheatin-az, Dumb-az, Drunk-az, Cheap-az, Lockedup-az, Goodfornothingaz, Lazyaz and especially his third cousin Beatinyouaz. Wait on your Boaz and make sure he respects Yoaz! -Unknown

AMANDA SHARP

Journal
Insight • Answers • Downloads
AHA's • Wisdom • Findings

SMALL **TALL** *tales*

NOSE PIERCING? SURE WHY NOT.

So one day I decided, with a great friend of mine, to get my nose pierced. I was thirty nine years old, single mom, and had always wanted it. When I went into the tattoo shop, the guy had me pierced and paid in less than five minutes. I screamed an inappropriate word and we left. What I didn't think through was that it's not just skin like your ear, it is cartilage.

Once I took it out so I could clean my face really well cause I had a zit next to my piercing. Yes, even at thirty nine, you get imperfections, its ungodly really. When I went to put it back in I couldn't believe it had closed up so quickly. Or the skin and the hole in the cartilage wasn't meeting up. Bottom line, I was trying to put earring in the zit hole. I pushed it through and re-pierced my cartilage as well. The noise and the pain was so bad I fainted. After coming to, my boy said "mom I really think you look pretty without the earring. I really don't appreciate you fainting and expecting me to know what to do." I'm thankful he didn't call 911. That would have been expensive to say the least.

After months of snagging it on my blanket at night and feeling like I had a goiter on the side of my face, I chose to take it out and let it heal up. I do miss it but come on, it's just not worth the pain. After talking to a few people about piercings, it sounds like mine hurt all the time cause it was pierced through a nerve. Hmmm, makes sense. Where in life do we choose to suffer because we kind of like it? We don't want to get rid of that item, negative person or ailment that we could cure if we responded to how it really made us feel. If you need a more tangible way to grasp this concept go ahead and pierce your nose with a toothpick and think about my question above.

Unleash Your LAUGHTER

You know that moment when you send a text to the dude that doesn't want you, based on results? That sinking feeling of "oh crap?" I thought I would start up a new business, where you text me exactly what you want to say to that dude that isn't even close to what awesome looks like for you. I will then respond with something humorous, real and over the top informational to cure you from your loneliness. Then you can go about your day walking in completeness, favor and joy. Team player right der. #curinghormonalembalancesoneatatime. This has been huge in my life to have my friend Cory respond to these rants with absolute truth and it quite frankly cures it immediately.

Email me if you are struggling in this area, I have got the cure. sharpdesignsinc@mac.com

AMANDA SHARP

JUST FOR TODAY
CAN I GET OFF THIS PENDULUM SWING?

Wow, after bringing truth to the light, watch out folks, you will be tested. Well, that I was, and the Pendulum swung baby! It swung back so far, I thought I was in high school again. It was eeerrrry and somewhat familiar.

So what is the struggle this week? One, I heard if you are in a struggle, you are still alive and God's not done. I'm alive and I know God's not nearly done, I'm sure of that. The struggle for me the past few weeks have been temptations of the flesh. It has been in all areas really, but mostly in the area of intimacy and the need to feel loved. When I focus on what I have left from a victim standpoint, it is grim. So, I meddled in that, on and off, the whole week. I chose to believe all the lies about my future and what it didn't have for me.

Here's the thing, one of my goals is to show my boys the love of God. Well, what better time then to be a walking sermon and billboard for them, through this trial called "divorce?" They will know God through what I choose just in this situation. Believe me, the lie that I am not important to the men in my life has caused me to doubt God's love for me. This greatly burdens me and creates a space of change that I want to walk into.

What has come up for me, is grieving the loss of my dreams and future. What that has looked like is a NEED, if you will, to fill that cavern quickly with something. For me, that is attention. I've never really been a girl to look for attention by how I dress. I would say the five pairs of Crocs would put that into perspective. I have however, plunged into my talents lately of humor and perversion. This is super dangerous for me because it is a counterfeit of my gift of joy, encouragement and laughter.

Some of my friends in my inner circle have whiplash with the pendulum swing I have been on before. We have laughed so much and so hard that my heart hurts. Some of it is good, and most of it counterfeit. I want to be seen, I want to share my life with people, I want to be cherished, I want to be loved. I don't want my eulogy to be my friends standing up and saying, "she was one funny girl." Nah, there is more to me than that. My playing small doesn't serve anyone. What is really detestable, is when I create the space for others to play small in their lives.

I realized that the coarse joking, literally creates a space for all of us to not be, the best. I know the reason I love my friends (male & female), is because we do experience great laughter. When I step into full perverse joking, am I using them to fill a void? I completely miss their pain and the gift of sharing this journey with them. Does this mean I'll never joke or be a pervert again, well, I'm afraid I'd be lying if I said yes. I will strive, with God's gentle nudge, to use my gifts to breathe life and not death into people. Be very clear, humor and laughter is a gift, there is just always a line, a counterfeit and/or pendulum.

When this happens, I have to take a moment and ask for forgiveness for my actions. I have down graded them and myself through my humor. My need to be loved was overpowering in the moment. I don't want to be in the way of what God is growing in each one of them and in myself. It is a counterfeit of love. I loved the scripture I've gotten when God so kindly tugged on my heartstrings on this subject, "You are better than this, come back to me."

"There's trouble ahead when you live only for the approval of others, saying what flatters them, doing what indulges them. Popularity contests are not truth contests." – The Message

Be imitators of God, therefore, as dearly loved children and live a life of love, just as Christ loved us and gave himself up for us as a fragrant offering and sacrifice to God. But among you there must not be even a hint of sexual immorality, or of any kind of impurity, or of greed, because these are improper for God's holy people. Nor should there be obscenity, foolish talk or coarse joking, which are out of place, but rather thanksgiving. For of this you can be sure: No immoral, impure or greedy person--such a man is an idolater--has any inheritance in the kingdom of Christ and of God. Let no one deceive you with empty words, for because of such things God's wrath comes on those who are disobedient. Therefore do not be partners with them. For you were once darkness, but now you are light in the Lord. Live as children of light. – Ephesians 5:1-8 NIV Bible

His personal words to me were – "Beloved, stop searching for counterfeit love, stop degrading yourself and others in coarse jesting, stop leaching their love to fill a void only I can fill."

What's your point God? LOL. Okay, I am in need of a lot of help.

I have literally struggled with what comes out of my mouth my whole life. I'm sure I've hurt a lot of people along the way. I also believe I've learned from each encounter that I'm made aware of. I desire to be free from this "addiction." In fact, when on a microphone, I don't fear what people are thinking of me, I fear what I will say that I can't take back. Some of you are laughing inside about my microphone mishaps. Let me stop here. Some of you have told me you get cold sweats when you read my style of writing. The truth is a dangerous thing eh? That's what the enemy says. I feel the most freedom when I am in the truth, HIS truth, covered in HIS love. God created me to be in the truth, the light.

My vision around the ranch is about truth. I can't set anyone free from bondage, but I certainly can have the guts to talk about mine and talk about how I could only do this with God. Do you know how many people you set free when you expose your ugly, degrading, sinful truth? Just to have someone say out loud, "I've been through that." Often times, they are saying "If they can have freedom, maybe I can too." I've experienced feedback on how my shares have created freedom and healing in their lives and that has truly humbled me. Keep going, your past is not who you are. Remember, the past was a minute ago.

--Meanwhile back at the ranch--

We have spent many years on this ranch dream, and now we are doing it without my husband. My step dad, an integral piece to this puzzle, is going through Chemo this week and my mom and I are at a loss for words. How do you explain any of this? This was not OUR plan God, what are you doing? I get to look at that anger and release it to God again and again. It is truly about the journey and I cherish what God has taught me so far. God has us in His hands. I am not God, and I can't control anything. I must choose daily to surrender to not knowing ANY outcome for myself. This failure of love (divorce) is out there and now I get to decide. Am I going to do the victim pendulum swing and create more loss and sabotage, or get grounded and centered in the truth?

The truth is, I am loved and He has me here JUST FOR TODAY. God has opened up abundance and provision for me that I've never created by my own doing. I was even allowed the opportunity to choose truly into this dream financially. I had enrolled others in to the vision but hadn't taken the scary step financially for myself, especially with no understanding of what God is doing. I got to allow God to prove me wrong. I put half of my earnings into Legacy this week. Time to put some skin into this dream. Again, how can I ask others to believe it is going to happen until I believe it is? Put your money where you big, fat, smoke blowing, mouth is, right? He asks us to move and when we do, His favor is on us.

Here I am, I am here,
Following God or drowning in fear
Here I am, I am here,
Choosing Life which I hold so dear
Here I am, This is me
This is my reality
Growth Growth Growth
Or just decay
Its up to me
What I choose this day.
Focus on the good, Or the bad
Either way I will be had -Amanda

Action · Growth · Awareness

1. Listen to the song – <u>Just for today</u> by India Arie

2. Listen to <u>Rescue</u> by Jared Anderson

3. What do you believe are your gifts and what is the counterfeit of those gifts?

4. Read Ephesians 5:1-21 – Journal your emotional response to reading it.

5. Where are you on a pendulum that is not serving you?

6. Who are you using as a "void filler" instead of allowing God to fill you up?

7. On a scale of 1 to 10 how important is the approval of man (humans/people)?

AMANDA SHARP

Journal
**Insight • Answers • Downloads
AHA's • Wisdom • Findings**

SMALL **TALL** *tales*

CALL ME MAYBE?

Here is another example of how someone with humor goes about their day. When you see humor in everything, my experience is that the wit train can be taken at any time. I usually go about my day and a song will come on while I am passing by a regular occurrence. Then, with the song in my head, I re-create all the words to the music. It flows (no pun intended) easily and makes me LOL all by myself. Since I don't like LOLing all by myself, I quickly post on Facebook to share with my "friends."

I passed by this dog in the shameful stance with shaky legs and abs clenching. Yes, the stance that helps your dog relieve himself quickly so you can get back to your day. The owner stood with a used bag over his hand looking the other way. Everyone that drives by knows that he's going to walk away and never pick up the hot gift about to be given. The dog makes it last several minutes because he's still pissed about the night before, left outside for hours. If he is going to feel shame and be put in a position to "pinch a loaf" on the busiest street in the neighborhood, then he will make his owner wait. In fact, the dog takes time to think about the Shih Tzu passing by with the lyrics running thru his head. Sung to the song <u>Call me maybe</u> by Carly Rae Jepsen

I threw a wish and a smell,
Don't ask me, I'll never tell
I looked to you as it fell,
But now its in my way
I'd trade my bowl for a wish,
Dingle berries for a kiss
I was looking for this,
But now its in my way
Your stare was holdin',
Big shame I was showin'
Hot pile, wind was blowin'
Where do you think you're going, baby?
Hey, I just met you,
And this is crazy,
But I just did a number,
So call me, maybe?
It's hard to look right,
At you baby,
But I just did my number,
So call me, maybe.

THE FREEDOM OF FORGIVENESS.....MORE PLEASE

Welcome back to the truth train, where we jump on a truth and ride it to Humbletown hoping to stop by Freedom Village and eat some humble pie at Honestyville Cafe. I have been pondering forgiveness and how to gain it quickly instead of allow it to steal from me for days, weeks and months. I have succeeded with a few tough lifetime relationships in "letting go" and not hold that person in un-met expectations. Therefore, I am not getting hurt by them anymore. I was wondering how to recreate that for myself in my challenge of divorce….and quickly. Why quickly you ask? I have two beautiful boys that are literally watching how I am going to portray God to them. They are sponging all of the attitudes, fear, and inabilities that I am expressing (even just in my body language or shortness with them). Why quickly? Because PEOPLE ARE DYING quite literally - On the inside, in their hearts, in their souls. I don't want to grab on to the noose and let it ensnare me and take my life. That is what un-forgiveness is for me……and I choose out!

I will show my kids who God is and what he is doing for us as a family. "Give me the strength to be what I'm called to be, stand up when they can't, don't want to leave them hungry for love, I'm willing to fight and give them the best of my life." -- <u>Lead me</u> by Sanctus Real I stumbled upon this amazing thought about forgiveness (I'm clear who it is from, believe me I'm not tooting my own horn).

I AM TRULY IN A PLACE OF FORGIVENESS WHEN I HAVE GIVEN UP THE RIGHT TO DESERVE OR EXPECT AN APOLOGY FROM THAT PERSON.

Read that again, it is seriously powerful. Go through the list of people in your mind whom you have forgiven and with whom you still struggle. The ones that keep coming up for me are the ones thru whom I am still expecting an apology. I allow them to keep hurting me just to prove myself right (that yes, in fact they are hurtful to me).

If I am unable to forgive, then I am creating that un-forgiveness for MY SINS, which are being created on an hourly basis. I have to tell you I have been confronted by many o' friend on how do I have peace (in my current situation). I think some of them, deep down, are waiting for the ball to drop and for me to have a breakdown. Or at least that is how it feels. Well, breakdown is done, I just didn't tell you about it for six months. If I didn't tell you, you can make that mean whatever you want, I can't control that. The question is are you someone people go to when in their deepest pain and loss or are you so opinionated and judgmental that you don't create a safe place? The question of me after writing that is "who's face came up when I wrote that?" Then I get to work on that in the journal portion of my own book. Take heart, we are all always in "the struggle" with our shortcomings.

I have an insane amount of peace. I feel like I am in the "eye of the storm" and turmoil is happening all around me. That is so incredible to say out loud really because back then I was being tossed violently in the storm. What freedom! It is because I have grasped just a morsel of what forgiveness is. I am forgiven!!! Truly once I received that, I am able to give the same space for those around me. You can only give equal forgiveness to others of what you have received yourself. That is the same with giving and receiving love. Today with God's help, I choose to forgive my ex-husband. Although I don't understand HIS reasons, nor need to, I want him to know that I forgive him. I humbly ask for his forgiveness for any area that I created a death space for him in our marriage. I care more about the futures of our souls then I do to be in un-forgiveness. I care about what our boys watch between us. I care about being free! I will ask for help as much as I need to because it clearly is a challenging process. Thank you for allowing me to have another open heart surgery. I cherish the gift God has given me to slay "elephants in the room." The counterfeit of that gift is literally slaying people with my words. With that being said, I also ask for forgiveness from anyone that I have hurt, known and unknown from my harmful words and actions. Let's be free together! Truly take life seriously and act as if it is your last day.

"Most people say they are waiting on God, but I understand in most cases, He is waiting on me." –The Travelers Gift by Andy Andrews

1. Listen to song <u>Lead me</u> by Sanctus Real
2. Make a list of the people that you want to be released from – that you want or want God's help to forgive.
3. Listen to song <u>Forgiven</u> by Sanctus Real
4. Journal about how un-forgiveness has kept you in jail.
5. After journaling, watch video – search for forgiveness and the freedom of letting go.
6. Listen to song <u>He Loves Us</u> by David Crowder Band – if you can find the one with Jesus on the cross, it is a powerful.
7. Read Matthew 6:9-15 and receive it
8. Listen to song <u>Holy Spirit</u> by Bryan & Katie Torwait

AMANDA SHARP

Journal
Insight • Answers • Downloads
AHA's • Wisdom • Findings

Unleash Your LAUGHTER

SHAKE WEIGHT – APPROPRIATE OR NOT?

When this so called "shake weight" came out I was amazed and also dismayed that I didn't invent it. It is so perfectly meeting the public's need to show their moves and enhance their forearms. This is an invention that has stellar marketing. Not only does it make you feel sweaty watching the commercials, it brings this childish giggle out of you. Some people didn't even know that they could laugh until the shake weight came about. Honestly if you are that serious about life and don't see the humor in that marketing genius then I got nothing for you. People buy these tools as gag gifts or just to have laying around the house like a trophy for all their friends to see. This said item has brought so much laughter in my own personal life. Even when you take the perversion out it is still funny. Where can you take this plastic phenomenon? After much thought, I created a list so that you won't put yourself in a position of judgment. If you have no idea what I'm talking about, youtube.com a video for clarity. Now that I've done this study, I can't get it out of my head, when I am out, the thought "it would not be okay to get a shake weight out right now." I have wanted to give you a visual reminder and am motivated to create videos to save you from embarrassment. Find me on Vine under Heavy Deep and Real Funny.

Here are a few for you to visualize. These ideas are copy written by the way.

Dentist – obviously you would hit him in the head while he is drilling
Movie Theatre – especially with a full bucket of buttered popcorn
Zumba class – you know you aren't good enough to be conquering those moves and the SW.
Yoga – while in the crying baby position (or any position really). It ruins Chi and focus.
Church – how distracting to be trying to max your forearms. Jesus cares but not about your guns.
Public Urinal – It's important to focus on aim I hear, not your workout, hit that urinal cake boy, focus. Plus, the heavy breathing when your exposing yourself is not approved by the general public.
In your car – There is nothing more distracting then seeing this going on in the car next to you.
Child care center – just not appropriate ok?
First date – If she is on a first date with you, she probably already knows you have big muscles from the bathroom flexing profile shot you put online.

There are so many more that make me laugh. I hope you had a laugh too cause that's what it is all about isn't it? If you ain't laughing, it's probably because you have done one of the above and feel ashamed. Jesus take the wheel (or the shake weight) and help my friend out.

Action Step: Buy a shake weight, just the act of it is funny. Give one to a friend or just leave in a visible place at their house during a party. Text a picture of one to a friend and ask if they want one, there is a killer sale. Do anything to bring humor into someone else's life, it will bring ten times back to you.

SHAKE WEIGHT OR GOD?

The ongoing pruning that God is doing in my life is comical, painful, endearing and quite necessary. By the way, if you haven't noticed, I love run on sentences, they make me giggle, especially when I can literally feel the analysts getting out their red pen, going to their head and completely missing my heart. Which by the way, what is more important with a human? Understanding their heart or judging every mistake they make (in your opinion)? It says in the Bible HE will prune off the unfruitful in our lives (if we ask Him) and encourage the good fruit and be nourished. This is my understanding of my emotional state and journey at this time.

Just to catch you up.....remember the piece I wrote about struggling with perversion in my humor and that being my counterfeit? I have been told by too many people that I missed my calling of being an on stage comedian. The problem with that theory is, that I thought I could never be a "clean" comedian. There are some of you that haven't found me funny at all, either way, not my point. Truly as a young child my report cards said "hilarious but needs to focus on reading directions." I about died when my sons report card said "a pleasure to have in class and needs to learn to focus and stop talking." Basically to put it in counseling terms "Amanda received at an early age, attention with humor and felt needed when people responded positively to her." So I just recreated that over, and over and thus felt a false sense of being loved and needed. Eckkkk. Anyone feeling the blow of that truth? "whoooped up side the head," I said "whooped up side the head!"

WHAT WILL I CHOOSE, SHAKE WEIGHT OR GOD?

I have the most amazing team (inner circle) of friends that have signed up for the circus freak show as of late. They have come in close, linked arms and held me tight as I struggle with the amount of unconditional, non-judgmental love that they have provided, clearly from God. I have sucked them in to slippery slopes, I have cried a lake of tears, and yet they have still held on. I've even tried to be super creepy and perverted and that still didn't work. This time it hasn't been my desire to prove that no one cares. I know that's a lie, so I didn't try that one.

"Why am I telling you this and you haven't talked about the Shake Weight Amanda?" Ok, Ok. Meanwhile, back at Walmart, I walked by a shake weight and took a picture of it on my phone and sent it to a buddy of mine. We literally laughed and made hilarious comments about it for a full day. Start me on the wit train and I will go till that horse has died and been buried for a couple of months, especially if it has brought you and I joy for hours.

I then moved on to creating an alias on Facebook and only invited the friends that would give me what I thought I needed; acceptance, attention, love, and laughter. The whole idea of this is just crazy really, quite the slippery slope. Then I was full force with 20 video ideas where NOT to use the shake weight, including the dentist and in my Zumba class. You already know about this in the last thing you read. It is about that pendulum swing baby. Honestly, it is a brilliant idea and the videos were going to be perfection of humor. One of my marketing friends thinks it a million dollar idea for sure. Hmmm. If you take the idea and run with it, just donate 10% of your earnings to Legacy Project Ranch 501(c)3.

It is for freedom that Christ has set us free. Stand firm, then, and do not let yourselves be burdened again by a yoke of slavery. – Galatians 5:1 NIV

Then I got the call, the call I had hoped for my whole life, someone who cared enough to stand up to me. I should say stand strong for me while I was weak. The friend, inner circle comrade, whom was invited to the "special group" asked me "what was behind the group for me? How did it serve me moving forward in healing?" "Was I settling for my counterfeit?" Crap, not only words I had used with that friend but very good ones to reflect back on to me. My face was boiling hot, flashes of shame, and then honestly just a feeling of utter love. I was worth pulling the slip n slide up from the ground and left to a TRUE CHOICE decision. See, this friend has asked for straight shooting input from me and now I got to see if I can take what I dish out. Honestly in the past, even my own mom has said "you weren't easy to confront honey." That to me means, I wasn't teachable. I want to be teachable, so I responded to my friend, "you are right, I choose God, not the shake weight." We laughed about how funny this pruning actually was. Actually I'm still laughing because its freaking funny. When I got off the phone another inner circle friend called in and said "what's up Daimyo (one of the great feudal lords who were vassals of the shogun)?" I completely lost it.

The fact is, I am a leader, all of us are. One, where are you leading people and two, would you follow yourself? Before I went to bed at 7:30 pm in a sheer humbled, broken state, I listened to a recording from my third inner circle friend on identity. God orchestrated all of those conversations in a matter of an hour. In our weakness, not in our "puffed up ness," God can truly work in us and us in others. I have exactly what I've been praying for, for 4.5 years. I have a team that is not willing to live in darkness, entertain their counterfeits for long, show massive love and forgiveness, and be teachable with the goal of growing and desiring Freedom.

"For the flesh desires what is contrary to the Spirit, and the Spirit what is contrary to the flesh. They are in conflict with each other, so that you are not to do whatever you want." – Galatians 5:17

I always have an opportunity to see how far I have come. I know that when I conquer this counterfeit or at the minimum find the balance, that I will be able to pave a way for others to have freedom. The question I have been pondering lately is where is the fine line on humor? Honestly, in my heart of hearts I believe I have to lose myself, be a mute and run back five miles where the line is drawn. Who drew this so called line anyways? Is it actually there or is grace running me with a personal relationship with God? I've been over the line for most of my life. Honestly, seeing shock on peoples faces brings me utter joy.

By the way, I did cancel my alias and returned the shake weight all in one day. What is more embarrassing, buying a shake weight or returning it and being asked "is there anything wrong with it?" "yeah I used it for an hour and my arms aren't any bigger." I treat God like a shake weight sometimes when I expect Him to bring the things I desire right now. It takes more than an hour my friends.

Action • Growth • Awareness

1. How is humor serving you?

2. How is humor hurting you?

3. How do you use you humor? What do you get out of it?

4. Listen to <u>Revelation</u> by Third Day

5. Do you have a group that can call the BS card in love?

6. On a scale of 1-10 how teachable are you?

7. Are you leading people to growth or decay, death or life?

8. Get clarity on the counterfeit of your gift (for example, I can create laughter and joy through humor or sarcasm and pain).

**Step right up, go heavy, deep and real folks.
Freedom is on the other side for those that are willing
to look at the good, bad and the ugly.**

HEAVY, DEEP AND REAL FUNNY

Journal

Insight • Answers • Downloads
AHA's • Wisdom • Findings

AMANDA SHARP

Journal
Insight • Answers • Downloads
AHA's • Wisdom • Findings

Unleash Your LAUGHTER

WHAT FACEBOOK WAS CREATED FOR....COMEDIANS

When I need a "pick me up" I ponder these things: mullets, naked mole rats, muffin tops in short shorts, stained tank tops, Rob Schneider yelling "u can do it," a van down by the river, spam on crackers, tab cola, M.C Hammer (all aspects), grown men dressed in batman suits, mesh half shirts and the sun burn marks it creates, Adam Sandler in any movie in the nineties except <u>Little Nicki</u>, Plumber's crack, and plunging out my boys toilet again. What do u think about?"

Mom tip: If you have boys that pee on everything except the actual water in the bowl, clean every surface. If it stills smells like an outhouse filled by concert goers on a 105 degree day, then check to see if the plunger you use daily, to get brown votes down, is in fact impacted with surprises. That could also be what is making your house smell like an elephant. You know, the one that relieved a whole animal in your favorite place to relax. Just trying to help. That's what I call "a technical foul."

I was just given a high compliment! I am one of the blackest white girls she knows. Betta step back.

Sometimes in my room I wear stretchy pants, it's for fun. -Love Nachoooooooo.

Was going to wear my prom dress for this special occasion of my voice mattering celebration but I chose to roll out of bed in all my glory and walk to the polls, one block from my house. Watch out, those stickers are legit, I pulled off half my eyebrow trying to be funny. Vote, do it in honor of my eyebrow.

Lets take a moment to visualize what happened to me in yoga just for giggles. If you've seen the yoga scene in "Couples Retreat," then you know I was past my comfort zone. I don't need help stretching more in the "warrior" or "crying baby" pose. Namaste this! Discuss. Is this an area I need to grow? What would Jesus have done? Really WWJD?

"Remember if u don't vote you can't complain. Heaven forbid u give up your God given right to complain." This was from a wise and funny friend from college that had me wrestled to the ground and my face wrapped in his sweatpants he wore for 5 days straight. So basically, he is a big deal. I stopped complaining on that very day. (Paraphrased from memory which is questionable)

This status is going to be written will Ferrell style. "No sweet baby I'm not upset you slept through that puke fest, I wanted to see all the un-digested food you gorged yourself on at the party tonight. Mmmm green beans, don't remember those being served. Ill get it, u just keep sleeping buddy, I bet you are tired from your gluttony." Blahhaha

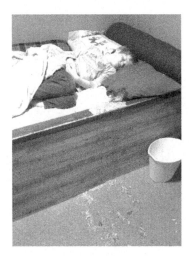

Movember isn't a good month to look at guys in general. Mustaches have always made me puke a little in my mouth. Great diet idea though, yeah nov is the month to lose weight ladies staring at that hair all scraggly on a man-boy's lip. I feel like I'm on the 80's throwback dating site. And done. One more magnum called and he wants his short shorts back, he said keep the stache.

This day is missing more cowbell. I wish I had a personal cowbell player that followed me wherever I went.

"Mom, what am I good at?" Corbyn asked in a sweet voice. "We'll your really good at whining and not sharing" said Tyler

ALL I NEED IS YOU

God has gently strong armed me, with my permission, through my challenges. Going through a public thing as divorce is raw, vulnerable and quite frankly, a stripping of one's identity. Who am I? What do I have now? Do I really have to be "on the market" again? Who am I kidding? Well, I am nothing without God, and these months have proven that. As the pendulum swings between stability and melting into a blob that can be remolded, my flesh has resisted the process. There were days I yelled "I don't want to be excellent."

Well, I can't get away from excellence. Not only is that who HE is in me, but I have surrounded myself with excellence. What a struggle between, I have a great "victim story" and I have a great "calling." Like one of my favorite songs says, "left my fear at the side of the road, hear you speak and you won't let go.....all I need is a glimpse of you.....all I need is you." He has a plan for me. Its just up to me whether I walk away or I take it on <u>with</u> Him. Either way is not easy that's for sure. The right way for me has been breathtaking, endearing, emotional, fantastic, impossible, outrageous and invisible. He is literally the lamp that lights ONLY the feet on His path. Do you know if He showed us the whole picture, our self talk and lack of worthiness would probably throw in the towel. "No way, I can't do that. That's your vision for me, seriously?"

"He calls me to the invisible, outrageous, & impossible because he knows I can't do it without him."-Graham Cook

It is the Father's love that draws me in. He is there supporting me tangibly through my friends and family as they choose to love me. He is there in my reading, songs, and journaling. I was lovingly encouraged by a group of friends to take a bigger step. I wanted to go into victim and excuses but really my heart (which is His) wanted to move, and fast. I set a goal and it serves me greatly! I set a goal to design a three day outdoor wilderness journey for Legacy. Legacy is the ranch (big dream) project to stand in the gap for people as they move forward. This is a huge stretch for me as I have lost the head of my family and have been wondering "what am I thinking." Well, ask and you shall receive. Actually, stay quiet for ten minutes and you shall receive. I woke up one morning and literally wrote out the skeleton in an hour. A couple of days later I was driving and He gave me a complete visual of one of the processes. I wrote as fast as I could while driving (you should see the sticky note I wrote on without looking down at it).

It is about identity and negative self talk. I know that every decision we make in life is filtered through our self worth. The people we hang with, the job we pick, the mate we pick, the addictions we pick, and the amount of death we pick. Well, how perfect! Not only was it huge answers for me, my heart could relate, plus I could pass it on. Along with an open, honest conversation with a friend, and a meeting with my core group about Legacy, I was primed to walk through this idea of "who am I?" The best teacher in my opinion is not the one that has arrived in a struggle, but the one in the struggle sharing the freedom they have found thus far. An open and teachable leader that heals along side the student.

Here is what I have learned so far.

I am NOT responsible for your happiness or if you are NOT pleased with me and my choices. I am NOT responsible for your disappointments. I AM responsible for how I perceive mine and what is behind them. I am NOT my relationships. If they fail, I'm NOT a failure. I am NOT my strength. If it fails, I am NOT a weak person.

Who are you? I can hear my friend ask this right now and my face flushes with resistance. Why? Honestly, I feel like I am going to give a wrong answer or that I will be bragging. Perhaps the response will be, "Are you kidding? you are NOT that person, look at how you acted last week."

"Shining a light into the deepest pit of your soul isn't the scary part. What is in the room with your soul is."
Amanda Sharp

In Him, I am beloved, cherished, perfect, forgiven, capable, called, passionate, favored, peaceful and captivating.

That is the truth and I can't deny that! It's what I choose on an hourly basis that matters now. This is <u>the truth</u> for me, and I have the power to choose this daily or not. Today I choose these words! Yesterday I chose these words, and quite honestly I choose these words more often than not. That is why I can get out of bed, get dressed, take care of my boys, be creative in my work, attract clients, have favor in life situations, and be at extreme peace in the eye of the storm. When I stand before the divorce court judge as he speaks over me that I have failed at love, I will choose His truth.

When I choose "death," I feel hopeless and defeated. Then I drag out of bed, am short with my kids, go into my counterfeit of sarcastic and perverted humor, align myself with the friends that believe immense lies about themselves, and drown my sorrows and fully "buy into" my un-worthiness. It is called CRAZY.

When I attended my twenty year high school, as a divorcee, I could have cancelled going because of fear of judgment. I honored my commitment and went anyway. You know what I found? We are all hurting deeply! We are perhaps helping a spouse go through cancer treatment, seeing a child make poor and unproductive decisions, or watching a mate choose out of marriage, and feeling the pain of rejection. It is everywhere!!! Pulling my "head out" to see others, instead of being so absorbed with my pain, was actually incredible. I had no idea that they had some of the worst years of their lives. I had no idea I was even noticed or even made a difference. I was a self absorbed teen, busy covering up my REAL self and in total fear of being called a fraud. At the time I did not know my "real self."

Action • Growth • Awareness

1. What negative self talk are you going to choose OUT OF today?

2. Listen to <u>All I need is you</u> by Hillsong United.

3. Watch video from movie Coach Carter – <u>Our deepest fear</u>

4. What do you think of this quote?
"One of the most outstanding signs of spiritual maturity is a controlled tongue." –Unknown

5. How well do you control judgment on yourself and others?

6. List 50 amazing things about yourself.

7. Which I AM NOT statements (above) do you struggle with most?

AMANDA SHARP

Journal

Insight • Answers • Downloads
AHA's • Wisdom • Findings

SMALL **TALL** *tales*

SPHINCTER TALES —MISHAPS, MISSES AND MESS
**WARNING: DO NOT READ THIS IF YOU DON'T FIND BM MISHAPS FUNNY.
EVERYONE HAS HAD A BM MISHAP SO LETS TALK ABOUT IT. IF YOU
HAVEN'T THEN YOU ARE DEFINITELY WOUND TOO TIGHT AND MIGHT
BE RUN BY PERFECTION, OR YOURS IS COMING I PROMISE.

In order to protect the victim of this story I will rename him Chad. Originally my book was going to be the title of this piece and a collection of stories over the years of friends and family mishaps. Aren't you glad I've grown up a little. Although funny, I do have more to offer the world. Honestly, I use to have friends call in to check and see if we had a new story for them. It's good for your health to laugh about the mishaps, misses and mess of life.

Imagine a construction worker all suited up for a long drive up to the site in the middle of winter. We are talking layers going overhead, covering Carhartt overalls, sweatshirts, button ups and zippers that are filled with concrete which makes them very hard to open quickly. I'm giving you this layout of the outfit so you can fully imagine when in a pinch, there is no quick way out. Chad is well known for his poorly working sphincter (a ring shaped muscle that opens and closes an orifice). The poor guy has "not made it" many-o-times. In fact, if I saw him sneaking up the stairs with something in his hand, it was to have the washer go to town on his latest creation. It became quite the joke between us. He always joked that he "lost it in the war," but he never served in the war.

After a long day pouring concrete in a remote mountain town, Chad and Brent jumped into his truck. The truck had been breaking down frequently and with fingers crossed, they headed down the dark, desolate road. You know the one, bumpy and with absolutely no light, pitch black. Chad felt the extreme drop in his lower gut, and that was not a good sign! You see, when your sphincter doesn't do what it needs to do, which is clench, then you have about thirty seconds to drop and squat or bend and release. Chad immediately pulled to the side of the road and jumped out of the truck. Brent, an employee and friend for years, gave Chad the "thumbs up" because he was quite aware of Chad's unique problem.

Chad pulled the first layer off of a sweatshirt as his head gets stuck in the small hole and he "Chris Farley's" out of the small item. Next is the zipper that is cement coated. "Damn!" Chad breaks into a cold sweat even though it is 10 degrees outside. He strips and rips two t-shirts off and gets down to the main piece, his Carhartt overalls. His stomach drops and immense pain shoots through his lower GI and bowels.

He stumbled in pitch black night preferring to protect his pride and avoid giving Brent a show. He was jolted into reality when his body is halted by a bobbed wire fence. Luckily, he was wearing his padded Carhartts so no blood yet. See, when you are overcome with this gut wrenching pain, great decisions aren't really made. Your one track mind becomes laser focused. He proceeded through the wire and completely got hung up. Writhing around like a trapped animal, the unwanted occurrence happened. Chad filled his overalls, boots, socks and everything from upper back and down. As his body relaxed in defeat, and he submitted to reality, the wire released him onto the snow covered ground. 'Now what?' he thought to himself. He was at least two hours away from a real bathroom. He had already used his last spare underwear and no toilet paper to be had. He quickly stripped down and used his recently ripped T-shirt to clean to the best of his abilities. It probably looked like a 2 year old discovering his filled diaper and making an art project with it all over his body. What I haven't shared, is that Chad has no sense of smell which caused him to be concerned on what others could smell. So with that in mind, he pondered the two hour drive home with Brent.

His stomach dropped again as he stood there in his half outfit and ripped T-shirt. He bent over and squatted in pain. Not the pain of the lower GI, but the pain of squatting down into a waist high sticker bush. These hair like stickers immediately embed into his soft flesh and felt like a million bee stings. He stands, and as he does, all the fine stickers re-track and get pulled in further. He screamed like a little girl, as his manhood was being attacked. He pulled up his overalls which included all the stickers that dropped in there as well. He pressed thousands of stickers into flesh that hadn't been abused that way, EVER. What to do now? Well, you take the walk of shame back to the truck and come up with a story that is going to serve Brent for the ride home. With all four windows down and winter jackets cinched in around their faces they drove back to Colorado Springs.

Laying in bed worried, I decide to call and check on his estimated time of arrival. No answer. Well, that means they are out of service and at least headed this way. Three hours later, I wake to a call. "Where are you?" Chad answers, that the truck broke down. "Can you call a tow truck or should I wake up the boys and come get you?" In a small voice he said, "I don't want to call a tow truck because I completely crapped my pants, the worst one yet." I'm pretty sure it smells bad based on all the windows being put down and Brent's head hanging out the window." Since this was before smart phones I responded "Okay, how do I find you?" A long pause. "Shoot I'll figure it out." He hangs up.

Apparently, God slipped a solid (bahhhaa, first one that night) Chad's way because the truck started after he hung up with me. An hour later Chad arrived at the house. I awoke to Chad tapping me kindly on the shoulder. "Hey, honey, I need some help after I take a shower, I think I have a few stickers in my back." I told him okay and waited for his thorough spray down to commence. As Chad laid on the bed in order to show me his back, I flicked on better lighting to see the damage. "What the hell? It looks like you are having an allergic reaction from your back to your knees." I looked closer and there were thousand of stickers puckered and hanging out of Chad's white skin. I proceeded to hear the mishap of the evening, the best he has ever told, as I handpicked out stickers from every fold a man owns. We laughed for probably two hours straight because, quite frankly, that is all you can do when it has to do with a malfunctioning sphincter!

THIS IS ALL THAT I CAN SAY RIGHT NOW

Sometimes after I write one of these, it ends up being quite the pendulum. I get a chance to immediately put into action what my big, fat, smoking blowing mouth, was saying. Minus the details and the blah blah blah, this time I had a hundred clients waiting for me to come up with a solution for a corrupted disk. When I went to fix it, it crashed my external hard drive. In the same day, the cancellation of a wedding was a financial disappointment for me as a photographer.

Well Amanda, who are you now? You say your work or the quality of work is not who you are. You just stated that relationships don't tell you who you are and you have some that have fallen away. I'm proud to say I immediately said this is NOT who I am, this isn't the end of the world and I have the faith to believe in God's only solution. One of my "pet peeves" that I abolished that week, was to relieve the pressure of people waiting on me to get something done. I dislike it so much that I over communicate to release the pressure I put on myself to get it done. Now!

Long story short my hard drive was restored after a week and new work came out of the blue. Thank you Lord for always providing for me and my boys. Thank you God for showing me that if I do have faith to believe, that yes, I can wait on you and watch you fix a desperate situation. Now that that was off my desk, I could focus on the core or the root as they say, of my pain. Now I can watch you give me the faith that you will fix my most desperate situations. Switch gears cause this gets heavy.

I have been writing in a personally responsible way about my recent sufferings and the struggle to stay seated in God's lap. Well now it is time to reach out for prayer. I have hoped that my ex-husband would reach out to all of you and receive love and support as well. The exact opposite has happened, he has cut the cord to his main life line (God) and all the other ones (you). This is where I get to choose again to trust for only one outcome for his life. Remember this is my perspective.

"Rest with me a while. You have journeyed up a steep, rugged path in recent days. The way ahead is shrouded in uncertainty. Look neither behind you nor before you. Instead, focus your attention on Me, Your constant companion. Trust that I will equip you fully for whatever awaits you on your journey. I designed time to be a protection for you. You couldn't bear to see all your life at once. Though I am unlimited by time, it is in the present moment that I meet you. Refresh yourself in my company, breathing deep draughts of my presence. The highest level of trust is to enjoy me moment by moment. I am with you, watching over you wherever you go." – Jesus Calling

I would love to know who has the faith and energy to fervently pray for him. I have literally watched him be completely broken, robbed, and almost destroyed. It is heart wrenching to watch him choose out on us, spiritually deaden, becoming emotionally void, and physically, to be doubled over in stabbing pain. I can't control any of it, nor want to. What I can ask for is prayer, prayer for a tortured soul. I can not stand here and watch the enemy take him down into the pit any longer. He does matter, and he does deserve to get help. He's not asking for help and I choose not to interfere, but to turn him over to God in prayer. His soul deserves this. Be very aware, details you share with prayer partners and whom you share them with, can sometimes be a fine line on gossip and actually hurt the person worse. Sometimes, asking for this prayer support and releasing yourself from the duty can be quite healing. I certainly have found this to be true for me.

This is when I am aware of true forgiveness in my life, when I can be in a place of sheer pain and still gladly choose to pray because a soul matters more than my own personal loss. —Amanda Fillweber

This is all I can say right now.

I included this writing in my book to encourage you to get to the place of forgiveness that you are asking and praying for the people in your life that have caused you pain. That you get to the place of worrying about their relationship with God rather then the perceived pain they have created within you. Love and Release and ask for support whether you are unable or unwilling.

Sometimes I want to yell, "I don't want to be excellent today" and then someone walks into my life that is choosing death, and I'm quickly taken back to my past of discontentment and deep sorrow. Excellent it is, I'm quickly back on the path of forward movement, healing and growth.

NEXT MORNING:

I woke up in sheer terror this morning, thinking 'what have I done?' Well, I know if I have fear, it is not of the Lord. Please know that asking for help and support around this has never been done in my marriage of thirteen years. He lives a very quiet life and was raised to keep things to himself. I, as you know, have been raised the complete opposite way of expressing my feelings. Please hold this entry very close to your heart, as he probably won't read it. If he does read this, then I hope he understands my heart and feels gratitude for my request. When you bring light to the deepest pit of your soul, you will see more things in the room than just a person. What is in the room with that person is the concern.

I hope when you read this that you had someone come up for you that you thought of the whole time. Take action on giving them back to God and asking for support and prayer. God is responsible for them, not you. You are responsible for yourself and what you are creating in your relationships. Death or Life, Growth or Decay.

Action · Growth · Awareness

1. Listen to <u>All I can say</u> – David Crowder

2. Listen to <u>Overcome</u> by Live

3. Listen to <u>Everything</u> by Lifehouse

4. Journal while listening to the songs about who you can forgive.

5. Who can you pray fervently for?

6. Make a list of those people and pray for them.

7. Make a list of people you are willing to release to God.
Be very careful when requesting support to be personally
responsible and not a gossip.
God knows what that person needs.

Journal

Insight • Answers • Downloads
AHA's • Wisdom • Findings

#raisingcomedians

"What's the worst thing you could drop on the bathroom floor?" My answer to Tyler was "my water bottle." His: "Open faced peanut butter sandwich."

First day of school - Tyler walks up to his new teachers, that don't know him, with open arms "it is so good to see you this morning." He completed the transaction with hugs. They both looked at me and said "that's the best hello ever."

Ty said from downstairs, "is that you with your eyes crossed mom?" I didn't respond. When I figured out what he was talking about I laughed very hard. He was talking about my license, where the lady told me to take off my glasses, I couldn't see at all and looked up to find what she was pointing at which makes me look cross eyed.

"What do you need Tyler?" "I would like attention, preferably positive." I love when people just ask for what they desire.

"Do u think Santa could teach me how to Dougie (a famous hip-hop dance)?" Just wondering.

On the way home from the pet store Ty (4 years old) says "mom guess what this guys name is?" I respond "Umm I don't know." "Dunkin!" "How did you come up with Dunkin?" I asked. "Well, he is brown and kind of reminds me of a turd." He continues, "Like a dunk in your pants." The car exploded with laughter as we thought to ourselves, "he has the humor gene."

So, I'm sure you are surprised that my boy picked Uranus as the planet he wanted to do a full Power Point presentation on, right? "Mom, no one has ever stepped foot on Uranus and it is definitely worth seeing." Insert creepy giggle. After letting him talk about the details he knew, I told him the reason that was funny to some adults, is because Uranus is another name for your butt. The turmoil on his face as he thought about all the comments he shared in class reddened his face.

So I'm driving with my boys and next to me, at a stoplight, is a guy singing and pointing to me attempting to be hot. Ty rolls down the dark window and says "sorry dude she already has kids." Insert jaw dropping realization that my kids understand a lot more to life than I realize.

YOUR IDENTITY IS IN WHO?

I hope to make a footprint on this world with my life, how far it imprints is really up to your interpretation. To me, God sees me and that is all that matters....or is it?

I feel the scalpel scrape across my chest once again as I undergo another heart surgery with God. My ribs are cracked and he is holding the only life I have in His hand, molding it, cutting out the death, and covering it with oil. This journey has completely busted up everything I thought was in order, my beliefs, the rules I've placed on myself, but mostly whom and what my identity is in.

My identity has been in Christ for most of my life. I'm finding out how small of a chunk I actually let him have and it was no where near my heart, I can tell you that. That place was occupied with man, marriage, friends, dreams, desires, work, unmet expectations, and mostly my self-worth. Listen, most of you would say to me "you seem strong and have it all together." Do any of us really have it all together? Let's tear the veil and release truth, so that we can move about this world with locked arms and find freedom and joy together...contentment.

Be very clear that I love the Lord and always have, I am just ready to take a look at the fruit. Is there any? Not based on my questions, fear and actions as of late. I took a dive off a cliff and fully expected the hearts of those in my life to catch my freefall and absorb me...protect me from feeling. Well, that happened and now my soul wants more, it wants everything and can't seem to hold on to anything.

A mentor of mine once said "the only way out of the pain is to walk through it." The goal would be to leave no residue on my heart. Well, now it is time to walk through the pain to freedom & joy. I have had tremendous amounts of peace and grace and now it is time to sluff off death and run on. As you know, when you verbally speak a quest, you will be externally challenged. I stated: "my identity is in Him." Guess what, I found out the exact opposite. Based on fruit my identity is in Man and fear. How people react or feel about me matters. I want to make a difference! The internal struggle is that I want to make it in God's eyes, not man's. If I walked in that, I would not vacillate on my dream but probably would have grasped it out of la la land with God's blessing.

So truly, who is my identity in? I have been reading and listening to a lot of teachings on this subject. It has engulfed me and I'm grasping for a life preserver at this point. I crave understanding on how I tick, I want to be fixed, I want perfection. He tells me all the time, "peace and grace, my beloved, you are dear to me."

"We are looking to identify with a person or group that accepts us. If you give me a little acceptance then I will become what you want in order to get a lot of acceptance. If we truly knew how much God loved us then we wouldn't be looking to anything to get our value and validation." - Quotes from Jim Richards teaching on Identity

I can see this pattern since I was a little girl. Ouch.

"Whenever a person tries to gain identity internally it always turns into some type of performance. It always creates a sense of rejection in us."

I have said many times as of late, I feel like the monkey with the clanging symbols, put a quarter in, let's see what she'll do next.

I do not understand what I do. For what I want to do I do not do, but what I hate I do. Romans 7:15

I'll leave you with this thought from Jim Richards. I still have a huge portion of it on my plate but most of it has been consumed into my soul and understanding.

"A person that has a healthy self worth is comfortable being an influence and allowing people to make their own decision. A person with low self worth is going to use power and force or anger to try and accomplish what they want to accomplish. Self worth is our emotional immune system. The determining factor of how things effect us always comes back to our self worth. If we sense we are valuable in God's eyes then that affects everything in our lives. The lower the self worth the higher the tendency of conflict and stress and overwhelm. Everything is personal and directed at yourself. You assume they are out to hurt you because of how you value yourself. The types of judgments are all about how you feel about yourself. Low self worth means you always judge that someone is doing something because of you. We judge everything based on why we think it happened and all that relates to how we feel about ourselves."

You are going to set your boundaries and dreams and relationships on how you feel about yourself. If you don't feel worthy of getting healed or happy, you will choose a destructive relationship every time.

Do whatever it takes to find your identity in Christ.

I just got done reading <u>Captivating</u> and am clear that no one except God, will fill that void I have. It is an octagon shape and I keep dropping blocks in that don't even come close to being the right shape. I'm settling on mediocre and I refuse to do it from now on, with His help! Pray!

1. What happens when you have put your identity in Man? What do you act like? How do you respond when they don't please you or do what you want?

2. Listen to <u>Sigh No More</u> – Mumford and Sons

3. Listen to <u>After the Storm</u> – Mumford and Sons

4. Listen to <u>From the Inside Out</u> – Hillsong United

5. Buy the book Captivating (now called Unveiling the mystery of a woman's soul) or Wild at Heart (now called Discovering the secret of a man's soul) by John Eldredge

6. Journal on where your self worth is right now?

Journal

Insight • Answers • Downloads
AHA's • Wisdom • Findings

Journal

Insight • Answers • Downloads
AHA's • Wisdom • Findings

SMALL **TALL** *tales*

GORILLA FINGER FILLWEBER

Side note: Just so there is no confusion on the title, Fillweber was my married name.

Sometimes in life you attract things over and over. For me, I attract and see the funny in life everywhere. I look for funny, I create funny and I certainly allow the space for people to share funny. I even became a "cleansing coach" because I knew I could create a fun business and also help support people that wanted to get healthy again. So basically, I have surrounded myself with fecal matter talk ever since I can remember. The setting for this tale is summer teen camp at which I was hired as the photographer.

When you partake of amazingly rich food for a week, and don't drink enough water, that creates one of two scenarios that aren't comfortable. The "Big D" or Constipation Station, both un-enjoyable. That week my lower GI decided to not release......at ALL. Well that is scary for a nutritional health coach, when you are consuming full plates of food three times a day.

I was pulling an all-nighter in order to get these teens their disks of thousands of photos I had taken that week plus create a fabulous slideshow. I had no time to have my stomach wave the white flag of surrender. I hiked in the dark to the less than desirable bathroom and hoped for this to be a moment I would remember, a five pound moment per say. When your stomach has expanded out like a pot belly pig, you know something is a "brewing."

I got about a 1.5 out of 10 on quality and quantity. In fact, I was dismayed, as I looked down and saw a basic rabbit pellet after five minutes of pushing. Now, I've pushed babies out, so I have the muscles to complete the task, but "no can do sister." I don't have time for this, I have got to get two hundred disks burned in less than six hours. I flushed, completely wasting water, and headed back up to my work area.

My friend Sheila took one for the team, and hung out with me the whole night just to keep me company. She and I laughed about my inadequacies. We had also made friends and comedy with the night shift guard which was a line backer shaped, hilarious, ebonic speaking man (seriously one of my favorites to harass).

Awhile later the night guard came back in to check on us and said "which one of you left the gorilla finger in the bathroom?" My friend quickly said "that would be Amanda!" After laughing at the oddity of what we were discussing I said, "honey when you have something that light, it comes back up the pipe. If my BM's were that little I'd be full of ….." From that day forward I earned the nickname of GFF.

THE WINDING JOURNEY TO THE END OF SELF

I was going to go to bed as it was late and yet God tugged on my heart to hang out with Him. I have felt at ease, calm, joyful and peaceful today. Nothing needed to be fixed inside of me today. Grace flowed through out my responses to life, and I am at peace. No real reason why, except I do know something has been missing for months, and that is the deathly "self talk." It verbalizes it's recordings of cancerous words on a minute by minute basis if I bow to them. I haven't bowed down lately to the lies, and it is really exhilarating. Thank you Lord, and tomorrow is a new day of choices. At least I have the faith now to believe, rest in my soul, is attainable, and I want more.

Lord, lead me on your narrow way (Matthew 7:13-14) as I write. There are numerous events that have brought me to my knees. I hope you will speak your heart through me as I write.

One of the biggest things I got from hanging out with a mentor family in Washington for a couple days was one question from my adopted dad, John, "what rules have you placed on yourself that keep you out of integrity?" The one I blurted out, with no reservation, was deep seeded and quickly found - "I will never get a divorce. There is nothing that God can't fix in me that would allow me to make that decision." Interesting predicament when the decision is made for you. I never thought of that as a child when I wrote that on my heart and built the stone wall one brick at a time. Well, the choice was mine. Whether to stay behind the wall in shame or to add a few bylaws to my rules. I have watched a lot of people go through personal development, and honestly, when they are out of integrity with even a grain of salt decision, it affects ALL their decisions. It allows corrupt self talk to come in. Lord, help us to locate the self inflicted rules with which we have cloaked ourselves. Help us come to the end of ourselves in order that you may prosper us in all we do in life. May it be a life of integrity and success as sin, self, and the world tempt us.

So I planned a skydiving trip with a couple of my cherished friends in November. Why? I love making memories with my close friends. Honestly, cause I'm open to seeing exactly how I show up in new circumstances. Put yourself in a "boiling pot" and see what comes to the surface. It is a great gauge to see where you are at in your faith and your self. At any given moment like that, ANYTHING can show up.

I had an absolute blast with my guide. We joked non-stop the whole way. In fact, I had a moment on the plane where I said to myself, I'm literally in a trusting, calm and peaceful state. No butterflies or sheer fear coming up for me. Was I that in control of my mind and emotions? I was partially controlled by humor and partially by a desire to be seen as fearless, not "girly." I had prayed about whether to go or not. I had a peace about it, but mostly I trusted that I heard God correctly. I asked for a huge revelation through the experience.

We did the free fall and the ice in the air beat my body and face harshly, pushing my glasses up on my forehead. A lot like the world eh? Creating blindsides and abuse to our minds and bodies? The parachute opened and I realized I had no fear. This was a miracle because in my life, fear literally has commanded my attention most of the time. The guide let me control the parachute which was awesome. Another parallel to how Jesus works with me. When I ask, I trust, and He let's me walk the path with Him. As the guide started un-clipping our connection to each other thousands of feet in the air, I yelled "do not leave me!!!" I startled my guide, as I had been really fun and brave up to that point. He spoke life over me and assured me he wasn't leaving. Interesting what comes up when you are in the fire eh? What was really amazing was God was there. He will never leave me or forsake me. Humans will come and go, but He won't do either. If you have faith to see God in situations, you will see him everywhere. If you chose the opposite, you will see death everywhere.

That was an amazing experience and I'm so glad I gave myself the grace and permission to have fun and experience life. HE is my tandem guide and the journey to the end of my self is painful, scary, and amazing all at the same time. I will close out with this reading from "Jesus Calling" which God gave to me before writing this. I believe it will uplift you in the space you are in right now and spur you on.

"My plan for your life is unfolding before you. Sometimes, the road you are traveling seems blocked, or it opens up so painfully slowly that you must hold yourself back. Then, when time is right, the way before you suddenly clears--through no effort of your own. What you have longed for and worked for I present to you freely, as pure gift. You feel awed by the ease with which I operate in the world, and you glimpse my power and glory. Do not fear your weakness, for it is the stage on which my power and glory perform most brilliantly. As you persevere along the path I have prepared for you, depending on my strength to sustain you, expect to see miracles--and you will. Miracles are not always visible to the naked eye, but those who live by faith can see them clearly. Living by faith, rather than sight, enables you to see my glory.

Legacy Ranch will be an absolute miracle! I am watching in awe as it unfolds with ease as we glimpse at HIS power and glory instead of jam our folded arms in discontentment and selfish impatience. It will be better than we ever imagined and it will all be to his glory.

Action • Growth • Awareness

1. Listen to <u>Healer</u> by Kari Jobe

2. What rules did you say you would never do & know keep you out of integrity with yourself?

3. Read Hebrews 4:1-10, write what you get personally from this.

4. Buy the Devotional <u>Jesus Calling</u> by Sarah Young and <u>Utmost for His Highest</u> by Oswald Chambers

5. Journal about what plans you are waiting to unfold?

6. When was the last time you fervently prayed on any subject?

7. Have you ever done prayer journaling? This is where you write out all your questions for God. Leave space and read the Bible, Devotionals etc. until you get the scriptures that you feel strongly are the answers. This will build your faith in God tremendously. He does answer those whom ask.

Journal
Insight • Answers • Downloads
AHA's • Wisdom • Findings

Journal
Insight • Answers • Downloads
AHA's • Wisdom • Findings

Unleash Your LAUGHTER

MY INFAMOUS FACEBOOK STATUS
& THINGS I PONDER

You're only as old as u feel, said every "cougar" still alive.

Have you ever spontaneously chosen to do something that may or may not make you fearful? On several occasions I will just say OK. I have grabbed a bearded dragon out of a child's cage with his nine year old supervision. At a carnival for kids, I asked the reptile guy if I could hold the hundred pound anaconda snake around my neck.

Me: "Ty get your backpack on." Ty: "this is me falling asleep on our conversation." I look over and he has his head on his shoulder with his eyes shut. Guess I won't teach the phrase "nag much?"

Between the Victoria Secret, Old Spice and Axe commercials, I'm pretty clear about why people feel discontent with their bodies. I wrote that while I was eating a fudge brownie and wearing my tired spandex.

Just scheduled a photo shoot cause I was told I'm better than Walmart! My prices aren't, but man will I make you laugh. Sorry no fake Santa backdrops Fo me.

I just missed my mouth brushing my teeth and spread toothpaste across my face. Good news is I get to share it on Facebook, as an important status and second, I have a tingling cheek of minty freshness."

Just talked with my mom about how we were getting from airport to condo - Me – "What if the sex trade dudes pick us up instead of the hotel?" Mom – "You're not young enough Amanda". Booyah 40th birthday pre celebration is off to a stellar start. That mom of mine, she so funny. See that's why I didn't try out for American Idol, I have family that tells the truth. Lol"

When I was young, my mom raised me to ask for attention rather than create negative. I would simply say "mom I need attention" and she would stop and I would sit on her lap. I still do this just for humor now, as it is fun to sit on her lap and I get attention, even at forty. Sometimes I like to create that on Facebook as well. Here is a list of things you can post when you are in need of attention.

RUN WITH PATIENCE

Well, I definitely know what it feels like to fly solo (make many choices without God and completely honor my flesh). Grasping air and filling those voids for a couple weeks now. I finally came to terms with the anger I was feeling toward God, but not wanting to admit it out loud. I've been in limbo for a long time, the rug pulled out from under me, and wanting to ALWAYS see the positive spin on it. God makes good out of the most desolate situations for sure. I have seen Him greatly move this in my circumstances. I know HE is there. I just truly do not know what to do with the mundane part of life. My mom just told me once, "you have a fear of being bored." Again, the deep end analogy which my book is named after. I do have a fear of being bored. I have a fear of missing the mark out of stubborn stupidity. I have a fear of discontentment. Fear is not of the Lord I'm clear, and I definitely bought the T-shirt this week.

Between the surprise of Whitney Houston's death, (she had all the world offered, and was still discontent), my twin friends hurt in a bad accident, and the bad news on the ranch financing, this week has been a downer. What do I do now? You know it is funny when I am in this mood, it is like pulling teeth to sit down and talk it out with God. Why is that true? I know He'll give me the answer. Here is what I got! I hope you are blessed by this too.

"Lay aside every weight, resisting the many temptations that continually beset you as you run with patience the course I have set before you." "Running with patience--in these words, I have combined the intensity of purpose and the quiet waiting on ME you must have, or else you will be overtaken in the race by fatigue of body and soul." --from Come Away My Beloved by Frances J. Roberts

Run with Patience? That is the most amazing word that describes the journey. Thank you Lord for that visual and word. May it not fall on deaf stubborn ears!

I've found in life most people "don't chomp at the bit" to have accountability. Consequently, those same people haven't achieved what they really want in life. "Just like a horse, blaze your own trail, and it is so much more enjoyable with a group." –Me

Watch out for exhaustion! When it is mixed with massive loss, the enemy cuts you off at the knees and leads you into fear, doubt and hopelessness. This is the plan: to kill, steal and destroy. Be very aware of where you place blame and shame. Cry out for help and surrender control to Him. We don't have control over anything except resisting the enemy's plan for us. Reach down deep, dig in, link arms and touch each others lives greatly. I lift my eyes up, because that is where my help comes from. My facade of having it all together does not serve me, vulnerability does. Give grace to those who have lost recently, shower them with the love that only comes from God. –Me

Action · Growth · Awareness

1. Listen to <u>Refuge</u> by Darrell Evans on repeat until you have a breakthrough

2. Journal about where you are at with God. Are you ready to release that back to God?

3. Buy <u>Come Away My Beloved</u> by Frances J. Roberts and it is to your resources to hear from God.

4. What has caused exhaustion in your life? Can you pause and see where the enemy has had a hay day with you?

5. Do you do life alone most of the time? Have you ever thought about your journey bringing life to others? Go out and connect with people, you will be amazed and probably blessed.

Journal
Insight • Answers • Downloads
AHA's • Wisdom • Findings

SMALL **TALL** *tales*

JUST PLANE ENTERTAINMENT

I travel a lot for my photography gigs and I always fly Southwest because they make it very easy and free to bring 200 lbs of equipment with me. I get bored by myself so I am always looking for comedy while flying. With Southwest, I get to play Russian Roulette on who I attract to sit next to me. I have gotten addicted to the "who is it gonna be?" It gives me great energy and hilarious pictures. Some are when the person knows I'm taking it and others are not. It quite frankly has become an addiction. I started posting them on Facebook and now have quite the following watching for the next creepy picture. People ask me if they are staged or done without them knowing. Really does it matter? I have to connect with the person and enroll them in crazy or get a natural rush to take the picture without them waking up or noticing. I have been told I have the gift of connection and influence, dipped in a bunch of humor and joy for life. Honestly, if it makes someone laugh (which I personally feel people deserve more of) then it is worth me possibly looking or feeling stupid or uncomfortable. Here is what I've gotten so far and it has been an absolute blast! Where in life can you make the mundane an absolute life giving, fantastic time?

WHAT IF YOU WERE EXACTLY PERFECT NOW?

It's interesting how God works with me. It is quite intricate indeed. It has taken me awhile to just accept it as the perfect way, and for me to actually listen to it. My way is not going to be the way He talks to you. What is easy for you? For example, I love journaling and writing so God talks to me through my writing. So when I am moved by something, EVERYTHING lines up with that thought and HE gives me numerous examples through several days. If I look for them, HE really drives home his point. It is ALWAYS done in LOVE and that is when TRUE breakthrough happens.

As I took on taking better care of myself (self honor), I found HUGE AHA's along the way. Imagine that, having fun, taking care of myself and God freely moving in and thru me while accomplishing my commitments. Can life really be this calm in the storm that obviously rages on consistently? I'm truly finding that it can.

The things that created this space for me was

1. Taking my boys out to laugh and enjoy life when I have a task list at home the size of Texas.

2. Watching The Lorax. Really getting the point of how one choice effects and kills off those around us. What happens when you allow yourself out of that boarded up house and TRY AGAIN even though you failed the last time.

3. Having a text conversation with someone that is struggling to believe they are someone great due to their past. Watching what the "NOT ENOUGH," lie is doing to people and being deeply grieved by this. In tears for them, feeling the pain, and knowing that no matter how much I say it, I can't make them believe it. Noticing personally it is hitting a "soft spot of pain." No matter how much I believed in them, in the end, the lie beat us all to a bloody pulp.

All of these things drove home HIS point today. "You are in your calling Amanda." I am called to support people to believe the truth about themselves and move forward into their dreams in order to greatly effect thousands. I have downplayed, and called my life mundane. Bought into the "I'm NOT ENOUGH LIFESTYLE, AND ATTITUDE OF, I NEED MORE." I have told myself it isn't enough because I am still not on the ranch. It doesn't look how I thought, so I must not be in IT (the calling). That is living from NOT ENOUGH.

So today, I choose that my LIFE is ENOUGH, and I truly have everything I need. I get to choose that I am an amazing person that has a lot of love to give and pour into my kids and others. I get to choose joy and contentment. I can finally say "It is okay if it is just me and my boys." This last year, I have been lost without my label of "married" and floundering. Why? Cause I believed that lie that I'M NOT ENOUGH, I need more.

I choose that I am blessed beyond belief. I have experienced unexpected provision in so many ways. I work with a company that supports people in developing self-confidence and become better communicators personally and in business. I get to travel and get paid. I get to love being a mom and be open to opportunities to excel at it. I get to take time and hang out with life-giving friends, and create amazing memories with them. I get to give expecting nothing in return. THIS IS IT AND IM SATISFIED. It is perfect. Could I have said that even two years ago? I didn't chose to see anything in this light and it greatly affected me. He can bring in unfathomable abundance in all these areas and it is WAY better than what I cooked up in FEAR.

I am blessed, SO IT IS! You have a choice right now to make. Are you going to choose there is not enough in life, you aren't enough and therefore no one else would be. Not even God. How is that truly serving you? Go blaze your trail, there are people waiting for you to show up in life.

"The pioneers are the ones with the arrows in their backs." --Erwin Potts

Action • Growth • Awareness

1. Watch the movie <u>The Lorax</u> – To which character do you relate most to?
2. What areas of your life do you feel "not enough?"
3. Can you accept the fact that you are perfect right now? It doesn't mean we aren't a work in progress and we don't need to shift into more healthy choices.
4. Who does God say you are?
5. What are you called to do? What is easy for you? What are your gifts? Start there, and you will be walking toward your calling.
6. Listen to <u>What Faith Can Do</u> by Kutless
7. Listen to <u>I Won't Let Go</u> by Rascal Flatts

Journal

Insight • Answers • Downloads
AHA's • Wisdom • Findings

Journal
Insight • Answers • Downloads
AHA's • Wisdom • Findings

Unleash Your LAUGHTER

MISC DEEP THOUGHTS

I just woke up to Tyler saying "that's what she said" "no Ty, that's what he said." Luckily, they have no clue how to use that sentence in a joke. Yet. Ah the life of my offspring. Proud moment.

When Snoop, Dr. Dre, Eminem, Lil Jon, and Warren G come up with a praise and worship CD, life will be perfect. Song ideas: Sipping on sin n juice, Drop it like its hot God, Snap yo bibles. Discuss.

During a real estate photo shoot, you can always smell, I mean tell, when it is a renter or an owner living there. At one, the realtor follows you around telling you that you missed the crooked lamp shade. The other, no one meets you for the appointment and it looks like a crime scene.

Seriously, does the ice cream man want a beat down? Is he smoking something, no kid is outside at 9:30pm on a school night. Is he selling something for the adults? Let me go check that out. Nom.

Saw a guy on a motorcycle with a baby Bjorn attached to the front of him!!! Really, that's okay?

I told my boys I tripped down the stairs last night and they just did six examples of what I probably looked like. I coughed up a lung laughing so hard. Protégés much?

Maybe the term "there are plenty of fish in the sea," to someone that is single, is not so great based on the ole Blob fish. Thanks for the encouragement though.

INSIDE OUT

It's time!! Time to lay under the scalpel and open my heart to the tenderness of God. Instead of duct taping it together, I chose to get the long lasting, life giving surgery scheduled for today. I hope you'll put on a mask and come into the operating room. You are certainly invited to join in, or sit in the waiting room where fear over takes you waiting for the news. Is Amanda healed or is she going to give up and stop breathing? We'll see....

If I am open to learn, there is an amazing revelation in everything. Sometimes I could write chapters because I chose to surrender to the process and truly enjoy it.

Awhile ago, I had the opportunity to staff an Advanced Leadership seminar again, and it was an amazing week. This is a heavy deep and real seminar, and I love every minute of it. This is the "refiners fire" setting per say. You dive in and see what impurities float to the top. Why would I do this? I honestly feel that I am either growing or decaying every day. **My goal is to build my character with God, not fix myself**. Believe me, this is a very new find, and I have found a huge freedom in it. Do u really get what I'm saying here? You are perfectly made and there is nothing to fix? (pause and re-read until your heart accepts and your stubborn lying mind submits). The truth will set you free and boy I am free indeed.

Since each of us has the capacity to lead at some level. This is an important concept to grasp. We all lead someone to life or death at any given moment. Our words can put salve on a broken heart or completely back up the death that is already tattooed there. Since I take this seriously, I choose to grow my character and thus breathe life into people instead of death as much as possible.

I use to live a life striving for perfection and stated rules. My rules were created by all the painful experiences I've been in. Then an opposite rule was written by me for my protection. I had expectations so unreachable, truly how the hell is any friend or loved one going to meet them? I couldn't even meet them, imagine that. Whoa, this is a serious revelation here. I am openly admitting to you, none of you "cut it" for me and probably never will. Don't worry I'm a failure too, these rules are impossible to follow. Do you get that we set ourselves up with rules that we can't succeed with and keep ourselves out of integrity our whole life?

If you are unfulfilled and you know it clap your hands? CLAP CLAP.

What an ungodly death trap! I was asked one time by a dear friend if I had ever experienced joy. I laughed cause I thought "what a dumb question". "Who is this guy, we just laughed for 2 days?" He said name an event? After much thought, I realized I couldn't think of anything! No accomplishment, special occasion, birth or amazing day truly brought me joy. Most of you are re-reading this because I have been labeled "one of the funniest people you know." The BS card has been pulled out of your pocket and is slapped up against your forehead. **Just because I brought relief from our pain momentarily, doesn't mean we experienced true joy right?** The ones who don't think I'm funny truly saw that I was robbing myself from something huge, healing.

I got to throw myself in the fire and see if I had grown in this area. Proud to say it was one of the most joyful, loving, forgiving, peaceful, healing and accepting weeks I've had in a long time. Friendships were mended, freedom was found, impurities were scraped off and easily discarded and healing was accepted.

I have found JOY my friends. The heavy, angry, biting sarcasm is not needed. The dripping perversion that ushers most away in offense is weak, and I am truly in my calling NOW. My calling is to be the best ME so that you can be the best YOU.

Thank you to those that have stood in the gap with me, held me, created the space for me to learn, and saw a greatness in me. There is something profoundly different now because I feel like living again. So those of you in the waiting room, some very good news is coming to your fearful hearts **if you chose to hear what the great surgeon has to say**. It was a perfect surgery and the healing time is instant.

Now is the journey of living, with no love held back, and complete space for everyone to grow along side me with full expectation that God has our relationship in place for a reason.

1. What rules have you written for your life that can never be achieved? Do any of them set you up to feel like you are never enough?

2. Listen to From the <u>Inside Out</u> – Hillsong

3. Listen to <u>Word of God Speak</u> by Mercy Me

4. Ask for God to really show you what Joy is.

Journal
Insight • Answers • Downloads
AHA's • Wisdom • Findings

MISC THOUGHTS IN ONE DAY

I just saw a guy with his finger in his nose up to his knuckle. Do you think he was trying the "swallow the sword" illusion trick for me?

Me to my boy: - "Are you going to wear those underwear again?" "I'm going for 60 days yo!" Like mother like son. LOL

Watching someone's kids play sprinkler at the kiddy pool water. Shooting it out of his mouth and making the hand motion of a sprinkler. I scan across the pool and see Tyler with a smirk on his face. I think I just puked a little in my mouth.

Using a dictionary for the first time since college and learning how to spell judgment, debauchery, epitome and other awesome words. Feeling smarter.

Side note: Self defecation is not in fact the same as self deprecation. I have used the first word most of my life. Even though its pretty much the same thing for me.

If Jesus was on Facebook, I bet He would never de-friend me or block me. He's that loving. I bet He would patiently wait for us to accept his friend request. I'm also pretty sure He wouldn't brag about His best friend to make you jealous.

One way pictures should not be used to teach boys, would be where a baby comes from. This in fact is better as a verbal description.

Interesting fact: I know this will ruin some of your stories you've told since you were a kid. Baby Ruth's do NOT float in a pool.

Proud mom moment - while I am eating corn on da cob Ty yells out in perfect Nacho Libre voice "get that corn outta ma face." We all laughed for a straight five minutes. "Haven't seen that movie in over a year.

Ty – "Corb guess what's better than yours?" Corb – "what, nothing?" Ty standing in the yard- "my milkshake, which brings all the girls to the yard." He continues, "Not the refreshing treat but these moves."

SETTING GOALS – TO DO OR NOT TO DO

A good friend of mine and I started a group in Colorado Springs with people that want to move forward in life. We would get together and share where we were at and get ideas on how to think outside the box again because we are stuck in some area.

Wherever you are at in life, find some accountability and move forward on what you really want. We can find plenty of evidence of what we don't want that we are creating for ourselves. Find someone who believes in you and wants you to achieve in these areas. Your life will be transformed simply by focusing on the positive things and your personal contentment.

If you are struggling, get on the phone and connect with people that can support you moving forward in that area. You deserve to create and complete goals.

If you would like to take this a step further, put a risk on your goal. For example, if I don't complete the goal by this time, then I will be cleaning twenty different bathrooms of my choosing.

I hope this encourages you to keep moving forward. I believe in you and your goals.

Great Questions to ask yourself as you set up goals

Why did you pick those goals? Will they serve you or others in some way. Are they out of your comfort zone? If you don't know how you are going to get it accomplished, then that is a great goal. Did you get kind of ill when you think about asking for accountability?

I can tell you I haven't gotten much done without accountability, including this book I have been sitting on for ten years.

"Accountability is the muscular hand that clenches the throat of the voice within that is saying "you don't deserve your goals" - Amanda Sharp

Action • Growth • Awareness

1. Set some goals for 30 days that make you sick.

2. Set up 5-10 people as accountability partners.

3. Accountability is to check in with your partners, whether they ever call or support you. This is your integrity of what you want.

4. Journal about why you haven't reached your past goals to this point? What stopped you? What excuses did you make?

5. Set up personal, business and family goals. Share them boldly. Your friends might have great ideas on how to attain what you want.

6. Set up Goals for a year so that you have big ones to work on monthly.

7. Celebrate when you have completed a goal.

8. Get rid of the "Blame Game." You have what you have based on results

9. Have fun doing it. If you are losing relationships during the process then you aren't balanced.

Journal
Insight • Answers • Downloads
AHA's • Wisdom • Findings

SMALL **TALL** *tales*

REALITY CHECK – INTERNET DATING

One day I decided to sign up for internet dating just to see what was out there. I have struggled with two thoughts on this. One, trust that God will bring you a great match or two, open as many doors as you can so that God can bring that great match. One idea served me and one didn't for sure. With my comedic mind, I was instantly intrigued by the humor of it all. I could not believe the profile pictures and that this was their "A" game. I was married for thirteen years and certainly understand when the lust/love wears off. The image of these guys in their old tired underwear, leg up on the couch, asking for a beer, is already surfacing vague and very real memories.

Actual profile picture that made me hot.

I got to work and wrote a very bold and honest profile stating that I was looking for "one" man not a plethora. I also stated that I was not a "booty call" or someone looking for the latest strain of STD out there. I thought this would weed out most of the non-options and maybe it did. What it did creae was a desire to prove to me that they were worthy of my time. Whether they met any of my requests or not. One guy asked me to call him so we could get to know each other. This is after two days of messaging. For safety and a "gut feeling" I blocked my number when I called him. He yelled at me "If you follow God and are going be filled by fear, then you don't love God." He immediately slammed the phone down. After ten minutes, he went on the site and begged me to call him back.

I was asked by another charmer "if I wasn't a booty call did I know more than one position in bed?" Um, what was your name again? I was asked to send a picture of me while taking a bath. I was asked what I was going to offer the guy if it wasn't sex? Is this for real? Yes it is. I am going to put it out there because I want all the parents to deeply and emotionally connect with where we are at in society. I was asked "If you aren't going to put out, then you better give good head." I'm sorry, cough. Silence. No words, Amanda really? I answered calmly, "If you knew how to treat a woman, you would get everything you wanted out of the relationship." "I am not your woman." I toiled over sharing that with you but I strongly believe we need to open up our eyes as women, men and parents. This is obviously working as a relationship builder. A girl has responded to this type of talk and therefore encouraged this man that "this is okay." This is a major concern people. At one point, in my journey, the enemy lied to me. He told me, "this is it, don't expect more."

Obviously, internet fishing wasn't for me. It was shocking and way out of my league for sure. It made me want to start a new program for teen girls and give it to them straight. Also to do a "scared straight" program for people on the verge of divorce. What was on the other side of the fence and why they should cherish and commit to their relationship. Gawd awful.

The profile shots that most men put up as their first impression was 90% bathroom shots. Where you can see the scum on the tub, the turd in the toilet or their hard bodies that they spent a lot of time on. At one point, I thought that I could make a huge amount of money and do their profile photos for them. Then we would be on a natural kind of date instead of awkward coffee meet up. I soon realized, based on response, that this was opening me up to a whole world of crazy. I didn't want to be in the middle of no where with a psycho that had intentions I wasn't willing to fulfill. Call me a freak, but I think God has a better plan for me then swimming in the STD filled kiddie pool that I was in. He has a better plan for you as well.

In the nature of who I am, I obviously got a ton of laughs from the profiles and pictures as well. I actually had a few girlfriends I sent the "dude of the day" to. When Santa sent me a message, I was done. This was a guy that played Santa for a living. "No I don't want to sit on your lap and ask you for what I want." "Hey aren't you married?" After surfing through hundreds of "selfies" in the bathroom, I added new pictures to my profile hopefully to inspire change.

OTHER HUMOR ON THIS SUBJECT

A guy had a total typo in his description of "looking for someone thrust worthy" instead of trust worthy.

Dating site user names I declined: thistooshallpass, strongrightarm, golddiggerliveswitholdwoman, healthyasahorse, kingothebooty, greatpersonalitynopictureneeded, heretoteachyouthemoves

DOUBLE MINDED VS. SURRENDERED

Wow, I still have staples and am healing from the last surgery with God. Am I supposed to write now? Watch out, cause if I choose out of being tired in order to have a relationship with God, then this should be nice and juicy vulnerable. This double minded woman is choosing to be surrendered right now. In my surrendered state, GOD shows up EVERY TIME.

So just for background, I have shared in the past that I have struggled with the mundane of life. The fear of being bored, the fear of having a dull life. Sounds absolutely nuts, but what do you do with a day that is cleared out for you? Do you question your whole life, your dreams, your laziness, your worth, ALL of your relationships? Well, I do!

I've had the opportunity since my divorce, the ultimate betrayal of my heart, to allow men into my life, or choose they are all dangerous to me. Since I lived most of my life in the danger zone, I gratefully chose out of that this time. I tried something new with God, and chose to love. This is quite HUGE as Jesus is a MAN and that greatly affects my healing process, whatever stance I choose. If He is one of them, then what?

When I say I let love in, I'm not just talking about ones I'm attracted to, I'm also talking about fantastic fathers, uncles and brothers to me. My life is FULL! I allowed love to come in to this shredded and once cold heart. God has granted me amazing, Godly, loving, and mostly Patient MEN. I say patient because, holy cow this has been a ride. You really have to possess God's love to hang with out with a healing soul. Or I should say, you have to be standing in your identity in Christ to be able to support someone who isn't choosing that. The opposite that can be created is void filling our soul ties.

As I was "fit to be tied" in my healing process, I felt like I was on the floor kicking, trying to prove myself the ultimate lie "I'm not worth you sticking around for." Well, you can imagine how this has played out in my LIFE and the NOW. Thank you God for putting those special guys in my life to prove that theory wrong, and to guard their hearts as well. Truly, a double minded woman cuts like a knife and pours the anointing oil on at the same time. IT's SICK and WRONG and extremely double minded. That scripture comes to mind again about "I do what I don't want to do, Why?"

WHY?!!!???

Strap on your seat belts cause the Truth Train has just arrived and it's about to DERAIL in a station called MY FLESH. What is Double Minded? For me, it is wanting everything God has for me, and being stuck in the NOW of what I don't have. It is wanting something so badly that I can't focus on anything. It is wanting something and not really knowing what that is, it is truly being in chaos internally and acting on it in desperation externally. It is something that makes my Beloved jealous as I'm lost in it, it consumes me. That for me lately has been specific relationships and the silence of my room between the hours of 7:30-

12:00pm. The place that use to hold love and happiness and now is where the jagged walls move into my personal space and absorb my joy, pinching out life. This is the room of loneliness. The scariest part is I've felt it married too.

I've literally laid there and felt a presence laying on my back and pressing my face into the pillow. The amazing part of this is the second I pray "Help Me" He shows up. This is how I personally know Jesus is invested in my life and we have a relationship. These hourly, specific acts of love toward me, that He gives freely and often are ALL received.

My soul sisters all know the extent of this double minded stance that I've taken for awhile. They have seen some sections of peace but mostly confusion. That is why accountability is huge for me. I have a place to honestly share and abolish the enemy's plan of me keeping secrets. These are the secrets we all have, where if kept will probably kill, steal and destroy our souls and therefore our lives. This group is safe and they hold the visual in their head of who I really am and how God sees me. They are a God send because in the honesty room, the living room of my house, all have bared their souls. Come to find out, we are all the same, just filling a different void. All the void fillers are just NOT God's best. We all know it and yet, in OUR FLESH we choose the FILLER. What is the answer to this?

You already know. Take a seat in HIS lap. I'm sorry if you don't believe me, He's there, always has been. If you close your eyes you can actually feel His legs under yours. He has His arms wrapped and crossed over your heart. You struggle but he's still going to be there. Can you feel the coolness of his velvet robe? Yeah the one that drapes over your body.

LISTEN. He's there.

What is the point to this surgery? Don't miss this in my back and forth writing. Stop getting stuck on grammar and punctuation! You will miss the gift.

I know who I am in Christ, and I have no clue who I am in my SELF.

Actually, I take that back, I do know the fruit of what I create in MY SELF.

Needy, wanting, disappointed, discontent, in a box, unhappy, unworthy, faithless, untrusting, unloving, selfish, sarcastic, perverted, mean, fault finding and just plain FLESHLY in all ways.

I would NEVER just leave you here as I'm not in my FLESH right now.

If there is one thing I have learned this year it would be this: when I chose to NOT be double-minded (wanting what my flesh wants and wanting what God wants at the same time) that is truly when God comes in and takes away the whole thing. The flesh drops into submission and peace is found there. Contentment. Love. Compassion for others. Perfection. He has even taken away feelings for a man and a future with him as soon as I gave it up. I want to be "seen" and loved deeply by a tangible person. When I give up that need, God takes away all the flesh centered requests.

How do you know when this shifts? When you're truly surrendered. The above fruit can NOT be faked. It is there or it isn't. So, if I am thinking I'm not double minded and I still feel chaos, discontentment and am expecting someone to fill the VOID and make me momentarily happy, I'm still a double minded woman.

If these are missing then you could be double minded in an area of your life.

But the fruit of the Spirit is love, joy, peace, forbearance, kindness, goodness, faithfulness, gentleness and self-control. – Galatians 5:22-23

"A woman's heart should be so hidden in God that a man has to seek him to find her." Max Lucado

Action • Growth • Awareness

1. Listen to <u>Whatever You Are Doing</u> by Sanctus Real

2. Listen to <u>Busted Heart</u> by King and Country

3. Listen to <u>Our God</u> by Chris Tomlin

4. Journal about where you are double minded.

5. Write a heartfelt prayer to God asking for help in these areas.

Journal

Insight • Answers • Downloads
AHA's • Wisdom • Findings

Unleash Your LAUGHTER

We were at the park and Ty was waiting for a kid to give him turn. He says "hey bro are you done swinging like a ballerina?" Seriously? Did he just say that? Now I'll know if he's punched in the face at school it was probably a poorly received comment.

"I am excited that this is the year to learn the recorder," said no mom ever.

You know its time to cleanse when your pants looks like an airport security guard's get up. The zipper is doing double time and the pockets gape.

Just got off the phone with a family member I have never met. Already emptied my bank acct cause her idea spoke to me and we're family. Greetings, I am Mrs . Asma al-Assad, first lady of Syria. The wife of Syria President Bashar al Assad, I have a proposal for you If you know you can do this, contact me via my private box: emmaasma924@yahoo.com.hk so that I can furnish you with more details but if my offer is of no appeal to you, delete this message and forget I ever contacted you. I await your reply, Regards, Mrs. Asma al-Assad. My heart really feels like we should all take a moment to send her an email.

For me it's all about the laugh out loud.

Good luck Santa, SIRI took me through the ghetto last time I asked her where to go.

Maybe telling Siri to call me "Douche Bag" wasn't a great idea. I was helping in Corbyn's second grade class when Siri was pretty new. They begged me to ask her a question. I mumbled into my phone and she said loud and clear, I'm sorry douche bag I don't understand what you are asking. "What did she say? Douche bag?" No I think she said "Dirt bag" (full out lie). "Nope, she said Douche bag." Anyways back to reading. I never helped again in the classroom.

Pondering the movie Fast Food Nation which tells about the disgusting miss treatment of the cows. I was eating a single cheese everything from Wendy's. What?

What does the pool, my son and a baby Ruth have in common? A fantastic underwater photo for my book cover!!

Is it wrong that my quickest wit and best humor is with my gyno? Hilarious! You have the choice to make any situation fun or not, suffering is optional.

I'm pretty sure I just heard God say "wait for it, waaaaaaaiiiittttt for ittttt.

SOUR FRUIT! WHAT DO I DO?

Since I travel a lot for photo shoots, sometimes it takes a couple days for me to get my head screwed on again. What I mean by this is, I've gotten back to some consistency with God. I have noticed for me, four days is too long without deep connection (really, I know 1 day is, but 4 is producing fruit that is foul). You can imagine then what 2.5 weeks will do? Instead of going into guilt I choose to live in the GRACE room. My favorite sentence to God is "Help Me." He does every time, every time I ASK. He is a gentleman and for that I am thankful.

So what do you do with sour bitter fruit? What I mean with bad fruit is negative thinking, bad attitudes and heavy sarcasm, the stuff that really hurts people. When this happens for you, do you go into the blame, shame and guilt or do you choose something different? What grieves my heart, is the residue of what I have created in those two weeks of disconnect. It is good if you feel a tug to go apologize to the possible "hurt person." If I don't, then what's it about? Well, maybe that is around PRIDE and not wanting to admit I'm wrong. What it really comes down to is NOT WORDS but ACTION. I can apologize all I want to band-aid all situations, but until MY ACTIONS line up with my words, nothing matters.

My favorite quote around this is..._"I'm sorry I can't hear what you are saying, your ACTIONS are speaking too loudly."_ -Unknown

I want to take you through something today as I feel led to. If it helps just one person grow, then it is worth saying. I want to show you how I roll in the God room. It is so intimate to me it might be difficult to explain. This is to encourage you to be open to hear God in different ways. Don't compare to how I believe He speaks to me, get excited to hear from Him in your own way. Accept that HE loves you so deeply and communicates with EASE to you. You have to turn your ear after you have asked him to speak to you.

I have enjoyed journaling my whole life so I feel I really hear him when I am writing. They, in my opinion, are my downloads from God, on something I've asked for answers on. It's usually something I am struggling with, with God. Then, if I'm open (that is the key) HE will give me conversations with people on the same subject. He will also give me music that rocks my emotional being. Sometimes the words in the song are so perfect, I burst into tears, because He is so intricate with me. He gives me confirmations that are ridiculous, like five books matching up in answers. Then comes the writing, and putting it on paper. Do I do it or not? Do I reveal that I am completely nothing without Him? Do I reveal my sin, my struggles, and lack?

Be CLEAR in this.....HE does the writing, I just surrender to the process. When I just start typing, without pre-planned thoughts. It is quite the out of body experience. In fact when I read back on these I usually say "I didn't write that." I usually play praise and worship so loud that my SELF can't function naturally or type out a clear thought. The reason I do that, is I don't want to write from SELF, I want HIM to write through me. Is everything I write from GOD? I think we are clear the answer is NO. Now you might understand why I haven't finished this book in ten years. I didn't trust that it wasn't just my thoughts. I do have a faith that God will burn away the human-ness and leave you with the truth.

So to wrap this up, I want to share the endless confirmations I've gotten around what to do with the sour fruit I've created. This brought me to tears, tears of joy. With a grateful heart I am going to present MY GOD to you. The grace FULL God, THE LOVING GOD. I hope you can open your heart to see Him this way cause it is so awesome. These excerpts from my devotionals were astounding, as they answered my questions and caused me to be peaceful and grounded again.

"Don't be so hard on yourself, i can bring good even out of your mistakes. Your finite mind tends to look backward, longing to undo decisions you have come to regret. This is a waste of time and energy, leading only to frustration. Instead of floundering in the past, release your mistakes to Me. Look to me in trust, anticipating that my infinite creativity can weave both good choices and bad into a lovely design. Because you are human, you will continue to make mistakes. Thinking that you should live an error-free life is symptomatic of pride. Your failures can be a source of blessing, humbling you and giving you empathy for other people in their weaknesses. Best of all, failure highlights your dependence on ME. I am able to bring beauty out of mistakes. Trust Me, and watch to see what I will do." Jesus Calling by Sarah Young

"Do not resist or run from the difficulties in your life. These problems are not random mistakes; they are hand-tailored blessings designed for your benefit and growth. Embrace all the circumstances that I allow in your life, trusting me to bring good out of them. View problems as opportunities to rely more fully on me. When you start to feel stressed, let those feelings alert you to your need for me. Thus, your needs become doorways to deep dependence on me and increasing intimacy between us. Although self sufficiency is acclaimed in the world, reliance on me produces abundant living in my kingdom. Thank me for the difficulties in your life, since they provide protection from the idoltry of self-reliance." Jesus Calling by Sarah Young

"God is the master engineer. He allows the challenges to come in order to see if you can vault over them properly--"by my God have I leaped over a wall." God will never shield you from any of the requirements of His. Rise to the occasion; do the thing. It does not matter how it hurts as long as it gives God the chance to manifest Himself in your mortal flesh." "May God not find the whine in us any more, but may he find us full of spiritual pluck and athleticism, ready to face anything He brings. We have to exercise ourselves so that He may manifest. When we realize this, he will make us broken bread and poured-out wine to feed and NOURISH others." - My Utmost For His Highest by Oswald Chambers

"Do not long for the absence of problems in your life. That is an unrealistic goal, since in this world you will have trouble. You have an eternity of problem-free living reserved for you in heaven. Rejoice in that inheritance, which no one can take away from you, but do not seek your heaven on earth. Bring each day asking me to equip you for whatever you encounter. Discuss it with me as you go. Take a lighthearted view of trouble seeing it as a challenge that you and I together can handle." Jesus Calling by Sarah Young

"O my children, the path where I will lead you is not easy for your human nature to bear. It is not a pleasant way, nor in accord with your selfish desires. I do not intend to please the self-life; instead, I will bring it to the crucifixion; for it can only be a hindrance to your spiritual progress and my working through you. You have faith in me; this is good, but faith with out works is dead. Faith I can give you as a gift, but the works I can do through you only when your ego moves out of the way. For they are not your works, but my works, just as

Jesus said, "I must work the works of Him who sent me" (John 9:4) Like a flood, I will cause the tears to flow through you and I will purge out your self-life, and I will give you my love. With my love, I will give you my power; then you will no longer be walking your own way, but you will reign with me. I must have over comers through whom I may overcome. There is an enemy to be contested and defeated; and to do this, there must be more than resolve in your heart--there must be power. This power can not operate until your self-will is out of the way. Yes, my new life will become yours in direct proportion to your success in emptying your heart of self-will. I know you cannot do this for yourself; but you must will it to be done. And as you will it, I will work with you and within you to bring it to pass. You will know joy as never before, and as never possible any other way. You will have rest from inner conflict; yes you must be delivered from inner conflict in order to engage in outer conflict with the enemy." Come Away My Beloved by Frances J. Roberts

"Do not search for security in the world you inhabit. You tend to make mental checklists of things you need to do in order to gain control of your life. If only you could check everything off your list, you could relax and be at peace. But the more you work to accomplish that goal, the more things crop up on your list. The harder you try, the more frustrated you become. There is no better way to find security in this life. Instead of scrutinizing your checklist, focus your attention on my presence with you. This continual contact with Me will key you in my peace. Moreover, I will help you sort out what is important and what is not, what needs to be done now and what does not. Fix your eyes NOT on what is seen (your circumstances), but on what is unseen (my presence). ---Jesus Calling by Sarah Young

"An amazing friendship allows you to ebb and flow through struggles and victories coming out stronger in the end. Only ones immersed in grace and love truly make it. Thank you to all my amazing friends." - Amanda

If you are saying "I wonder if she is thinking about me?" Know I AM. It takes a village to raise a child of God, I love my village.

Action • Growth • Awareness

1. Listen to <u>The Words I Would Say</u> by Sidewalk Prophets

2. Listen to <u>Let it Fade</u> by Jeremy Camp

3. Are your words matching your action. If you really want to know the truth, ask five people "Is what I do matching my words?"

4. Listen to <u>My hope Is In You</u> by Aaron Shust

5. Listen to <u>Jesus Saves</u> by Jeremy Camp

6. Journal about what you feel He is telling you right now. Just start writing and see what happens for you.

7. Pray Today-all day – Practice including him in constant gratitude and prayer for what you see He is doing around you.

8. Practice what I talk about in this message. Ask for confirmations in any format. Practice hearing from God so when you have a decision to make, you know His voice.

Journal

Insight • Answers • Downloads
AHA's • Wisdom • Findings

MISSION TRIP MISHAPS

With a humor like mine, it takes a lot to embarrass me. Because of that, people sometimes want to know what my most embarrassing moment is. Really just one? How about the time I yelled "white power" instead of "woman power" on the microphone in front of a hundred people. Or the time I tripped up the stairs and skidded across the gravel on my face in front of a thousand people leaving chapel in college. My top one for a long time, was when I got de-pants on the rings in gymnastics in eighth grade. My shirt was above my belly button and pants hanging off my toes. The boy yelled "Hey everyone, look at Amanda." Hmm, I skim through the rolodex in my mind of hundreds, most spur of the moment fun, others mistakes in public, and then the one came to mind. Venezuela.

In college, I signed up for a summer missions trip that would take us overseas. I was super excited to do this and learn about myself and share my heart for God with others. We learned to do a silent interpretive skit with music and words in their language. This told the story of Jesus' love through silent acting and music. We would set up on a corner and do as many shows as we could. We had great costumes and makeup. I had the part of a mime. We could not make any face except "no emotion face" and absolutely not move our eyes. We even did this at a leper hospital at a city dump, while the thousands of flies landed on our face and eyes. At one point, I had a fly land on my eyeball. I successfully stayed still as it probably laid its eggs or wiped its hands. It was a sweltering 120 degrees, which means not enough water, and not enough water means dehydration, which equals the BIG D (Diarrhea).

I was owning my part like I was in Hollywood. Sweat was dripping down my face which created a stream of white makeup dripping onto my shirt. The sweltering sun was beating down on our bodies and my lower GI was crying in agony. I scanned the surroundings and realized there was no bathroom on site for us. Ironic because we were at the dump. I should have just squatted behind a pile of trash but I still had some pride apparently. I leave promptly in the middle of the skit, clenched my butt cheeks together, and skipped awkwardly with my legs crossed off the stage.

Options were scarce, so I ran to an older lady who had been watching me run through the "barrios." She met my crossed eyes. Doubled over in abdominal twisting, I asked hurriedly "Donde esta el bano?" She grabbed my arm and lead me into a room in the middle of her concrete house. There were no doors or window coverings, just make shift walls. She lead me to the middle of an empty room with a bucket. I didn't have time to ponder or be embarrassed, I pulled a "Dumb and Dumber" scene on that bucket. I had a no holding back kind of moment. I questioned on if I actually passed some organs in the ordeal.

With no toilet paper around I pulled my mime outfit back into submission and did the "walk of shame" out the door, where several neighbors were hanging out trying to figure out what that noise was. I could look no one in the eye. I said "Gracious" and bowed. Inside I'm thinking, thank you for letting me completely ruin your house for a couple of hours and by the way, Jesus loves you. She took the bucket and poured it all on the floor which was slanted to allow all liquid to flow down to the canal at the end of the room. My mouth dropped in sheer humiliation. She bowed and smiled and walked away as if this was no problem. All that to say, I truly left my mark and made a big difference in Venezuala.

ENABLING IS A DEATH TRAP

If you're an enabler and you know it clap your hands. **CLAP CLAP AND 40 MORE CLAPS.**

Well, hmmm, do I want to reveal one of my huge weaknesses? This could possibly hurt feelings if I do, as it will bring an immense revealing light on a good majority of my relationships up to now. Lord, help my readers hear your heart on this, this weakness is mine. May it strengthen my existing relationships and allow me to attract more of what you truly have for me. --Amen

"My grace is all you need. My power works best in weakness. So now I am glad to boast about my weaknesses, so that the power of Christ can walk through me." 1 Cor 12:9

Recently, through relationship trials, I have had a ROOT as they say, come up that I would like to PULL OUT. I want to pull this out because it is a root that has constantly brought death to me. I want to work through this as I write. Please understand, this is just the beginning of my awareness. This is a very dangerous topic for me as there is a pendulum of healthy and deadly to it. In each relationship up to this point, you can easily read where I am at on the swing.

When talking to a couple of my "on this journey friends" about my struggle, the same thing kept coming up. "Amanda, when you enable a person, "you play God." "There is a point when they are strong enough to stand on their own and you get tossed aside, unneeded." These are powerful words and they cut deep. I thought back to my failed relationships and sure enough that enabling (believing in someone, when they don't) was there. Are you kidding me? My mind quickly rejected this theory because it's not a truth I want to own. There is also the co-dependent tie that I create to me instead of God. Not on purpose, but out of my NEED TO BE NEEDED. This is brutal to type out AND I'm a strong believer of bringing the truth to the light. I want to "pull off the chains" to be free from this.

The way I easily create this is that I am a person that people feel safe enough to tell me their deepest secrets to. They reveal it all and I then become a resource and support. I've been told I create a comfortable, non-judgmental space for people to talk through things. I love that I create that and it has always fed my need to be needed. The key to your gift is knowing when the pendulum swings to an unhealthy place. For me, unhealthy side of my gift is when it turns into doing it for them, being the only one they talk to instead of God and quite frankly "playing God."

Now, hear me on this, because this is important. I have the gift of encouragement (exhortation). I also have a strong desire for truth and discernment. By the way, if you are unaware of your gifts, there are great spiritual gift tests you can take to get clarity. It is a way of finding out how God can easily use you in the world. I also feel that my life calling is to support people into realizing the death of negative self talk and finding freedom in dreaming again. Stepping in to what God has called them to be. In my relationships, it is when it starts dripping with ME and my opinion, that I need to stop and ask God for help. This is a MUST for me to learn, as my calling to move youth forward is from God, but it doesn't include me being their savior. If I don't work this out now, I will be in constant devastation when they get strong enough to not need me anymore. I can see this with my boys as well. Isn't the root of having children because I want to be needed by them and they look to ME for constant love, support and guidance? Crap, this sucks to type out. Let me take a moment and pray right now, I'll be back, hopefully with courage.

As I closed my eyes and cried for help on writing this, I heard "To whom much is given, much is required Amanda, keep going." I choose to fumble through my healing, and I can feel your grace support me as I do. "Fear is NOT of me Amanda, move through this."

Okay God you mean to tell me, even going back as a child, I created relationships where the "under dog, the struggler" started as a desire to support and ended up "LEFT" when they were strong? This is devastating to hear God. I see the track record, and I see where ME came in, thus pinching you out completely. Since I live in the grace room God, I take that and raise two hands surrendered, ready to give that up.

I have to take a moment to ask for your forgiveness God and I know you are just standing there smiling and looking at me with adoring cherishing eyes. You knew all of this, you allowed all of this, and you've pre-forgiven all of this. Because this isn't about perfection, this is about character, isn't it? Be very clear, only GOD is the one that can bring this type of understanding and clarity on a subject which I'VE prayed and asked for answers on. He is answering my prayers.

What NOW? Now I have the choice to recognize QUICKLY when I create a relationship that NEEDS me instead of GOD. Honestly, as my friends read this, I don't mean "you've been a weak person that needs me." I actually love you so much and want to see freedom in your life so much that there are moments when I take you on instead of trusting God to bring you to health. I'm not saying that all my relationships NEED ME, I'm saying I've been attracted to YOU because you VALUED ME and that made me feel good. It's what happens when you DONT NEED ME eventually that has brought much pain. THIS IS NOT YOUR SIN, THIS IS MINE. I never should have grasped your throat as you grew into God. I honesty NEVER should have seen it as you didn't need me and now I'm hurt. If I was healthy and grounded in GOD, I would have rejoiced in your freedom and had the faith to believe that God had you. WHAT AN AMAZING LIFE GIVING SPIN LORD, THANK YOU. I know this isn't just my struggle, but that is between you and God to find that out. The fact of the matter is I ATTRACT like minded people into my life. I have amazing elite leaders and God fearing people in my life and we all struggle with creating co-dependent relationships.

I want to attract a MAN in my life that doesn't need me. He will be so grounded in Christ that he doesn't look to me for answers, he comes to me for confirmations on the answers he's already downloaded from God. I wrote this out because this is an accountability sentence that will bring irritation and change in the future for me. It brings guidance as I wade through the dating scene totally getting pulled off the tracks. I want a man that is so close to God that I can come in and be in that space and we can move together easily.

I challenge you today to look at the relationship path of devastation in your lives. Could it be that we are the common denominator and keep recreating the same pain over and over? Yours could be a completely different vice and the common ness that we all have is that we want to be loved and needed. Let's swing over to a healthy place today and trust that God has all of us in His palm. There is only one savior and its not us. He has an amazing plan for us that is already happening. He would never send a soldier to fight this world unarmed and untrained. He would also never send you alone to fight off 20,000 adversaries. We are in training. Go with HIM and surrender what it needs to look like.

I am so thankful for this as I have asked over and over, "what am I doing wrong Lord." Why does it always end up this way? Here is the beginning of his answers for me. In a prideful way I PRAY that someone else out there can relate to this NEED. Dear God, I hope I didn't just strip down and run naked through empty streets. And, if it is just you and me God, I will tremble with you and that is enough.

I am the life and light in abundance. As you spend time soaking in my presence, you are energized and lightened. Through communing with Me, you transfer your heavy burdens to My strong shoulders. By gazing at Me, you gain My perspective on your life. This time alone with Me is essential for unscrambling your thoughts and smoothing out the day before you. Be willing to fight for this precious time with Me. Opposition comes in many forms; your own desire to linger in bed; the evil one's determination to distract you from Me; the pressure of family, friends and your own inner critic to spend your time more productively. As you grow in your desire to please me above all else, you gain strength to resist these opponents. Delight yourself in Me, for i am the deepest desire of your heart." -Jesus Calling by Sarah Young

Since I choose to live in the GRACE room with God, I will close with this. Thank you to all my relationships that have brought this iron sharpening awareness to reality. I ask for your forgiveness on wanting to see your freedom so badly that it got warped around ME instead of God. Thank you to the friendships I have that have NEVER needed me and have only looked to God for help. Now I know what I can give, God's love through me. How easy is that?

Thank you for the space to heal, I hope that you find something for you.

1. Listen to <u>Light Up The Sky</u> by The Afters

2. Listen to <u>Word of God Speak</u> by Mercy Me

3. Listen to <u>Mountain of God</u> by Third Day

4. Journal about whom you believe you are enabling?

5. What is this creating in your life and theirs that is not serving either one of you?

6. What do you have a track record of doing in relationships? Ask God to show you when it is healthy and when it goes into "your needs."

7. Do you have a track record of being "left" when people believe in themselves enough to take on their lives?

8. Is your identity in Christ or the response of man (all humans) to you?

9. What matters most: what God feels about you or man?

Journal
Insight • Answers • Downloads
AHA's • Wisdom • Findings

Unleash Your LAUGHTER

MISC THOUGHTS AND SMILES

A thin rope and a hand or mattress wins going 60 mph? Just saw the height that a mattress can fly.

Does the 5 second rule apply to dropping a shirt on the shower floor at the gym? I think not, a bon fire applies.

After 20 years of opening yogurts, I still haven't mastered it not getting all over my shirt. Invention please!

Ty started talking like Adam Sandler. This is one of my examples that dreams do come true. "yabadeedoooooo!"

Cooked me up some honey badger tonight with a side hollandaise sauce.

Looks like a good book, the covers sell it for me. – Uranus

Is it wrong to rev your engine and make the cop next to me laugh?

NOW HIRING: mad skillz at the cowbell. Travel with me when I'm out and do your thing. Will Ferrell is too busy. Must have hairy gut and half sweater like him.

Just heard the song "you look better with the lights off" --not good to say out loud or write a song about. just saying

Corbyn just told me his two favorite faces that I make. It was hilarious cause he did them perfectly with hand signals. I guess I didn't realize I made those faces thhhhhaaaattt much.

Ty said opening to the whole family, "Grandpa must have fought really hard in the war cause now he just sits in a chair all day." Corbyn looked mortified and said "not cool Tyler, not cool at all."

"It's not my fault I'm cute, I can't change that" –Tyler

"Mom, I might be too attractive to be eating this zucchini." - Corbyn

When I was in Vegas I noticed the bus line was called "the deuce." I laughed pretty hard wondering if their motto is "dropping you off like a deuce."

Also seen in Vegas: A guy who's underwear was so tired and stretched out, it hung out of both leg holes almost to the ground.

DARK KNIGHT – DARK NIGHT

Waking up to early morning Facebook status feeds to PRAY feels familiar as we just got the fires put out in Colorado. What now? Honestly, I don't watch the news anymore. I really do get my news from Facebook. Judge me if you like, but I can't stomach 90% of what is going on in the world. I lift my eyes up because that is where my help comes from. As a single mom, the news actually strikes fear in my heart and I choose to not live in fear.

As I opened up the news link wondering what happened in Colorado today, my heart wrenched in pain. Another lost soul, obviously completely won over to the other side, taking it out on society. Tears flowed down my face when I heard the descriptions of the young kids that were there witnessing not only the movie but real life happening before their eyes. Innocence lost is extremely upsetting to this mom.

I've always heard that we are ALL capable of ALL sin and our minds are one shift away from disconnecting from what is pure, true, noble and SANE. The disturbing part is when something this hideous is well thought out and the conscience mind is that severed. They are calling this the Colorado Movie Massacre, where 12 are deceased, 79 shot, and at least 50 injured. **Now tell me, does one life, including yours, affect the world?**

Yes, you're damn right! All of us sitting around wondering what to do with our lives should be jumping out of our seats. We finally know we are of value and have a purpose right? No, you still don't know? Have you ever thought that maybe your purpose was to just LOVE? LOVE no matter what? It seems that is the most challenging purpose of them all. Do any of us really have LOVE down? If given the chance, would I turn and hug the shooter? Would I stand up and walk toward him as he sandblasted me with bullets just so I could tell him he is loved? Would I crumble with him to the ground and not release until his body stopped fighting and he owned that he was loved? Would I pray with him, forgive him and stand by him as he struggled with God?

The sad truth is, He is broken, and so am I in some areas. He is lost, and so am I in some areas. He is faithless, and so am I in some areas. He is angry and hateful, and so am I in some areas. He has done the unthinkable, demolished lives and damaged relationships, and so have I. **This act in no way is acceptable, or without extremely gut wrenching consequences.** Please don't hear I am condoning this travesty. I am also not condoning the sin in my life. What do we do in the midst of this storm?

If I truly have an affect on the world, what do I do now? What am I called to do? I believe as Christians we are to be preparing for this kind of loss. I could be so grounded in Christ that I travel to the site of destruction. I could be open to God leading me on who and how to talk to the people that are completely lost, angry and pondering on checking out. Honestly, the first thing that went through my mind was anger and judgment. I couldn't believe I was hearing that young kids were at this movie in the first place. Three month old baby to young kids at a midnight showing? What has this world come to, seriously?

The violence that we are allowing to steal the innocence of our children grieves my spirit to the point of tears. I'm so mad at all of it. The second rush of anger was toward the enemy's puppet. How does a boy get so lost that the enemy easily moves him into not caring about life, or hundreds for that matter. My first response to all of this is not love.

So what now?

What can I do now that I've released judgment and anger? Well, based on feedback from my life and my writing, I will reach out and make a stand for leadership in the midst of the storm. I am important, and I do make a difference. Every single person has a role in this shooting. We weren't in the situation crawling on the floor, being shot at, sticking our hand in a bullet wound or crying out in pain and agony. Think about it though, in some areas of our life, we are experiencing just that. The pain or circumstance isn't the same, but it is there in a disabling way isn't it? I think it is safe to say that the world isn't getting better ehh? What can we do in this fallen world?

I chose to talk to my older son about this shooting. We cried together and he started praying for the victims, no lie. I talked to him about some of the sad and angry kids in his class last year and how a lot of times these kids have very negative homes. As they grow up, their attitudes and treatment of others create a cycle of being left out and made fun of. The cycle repeats and you have a very angry teen that just wants to be loved and heard and SEEN. When they are NOT SEEN, they create more negative attention and get SEEN. I talked to him about loving the unlovable. What it means to be a leader, loving all and not getting sucked into the negative that they are creating for themselves. I remember all the ones left behind that I've impacted with humor and encouragement in high school. Seeing the light turn on in someone's eyes is extremely rewarding. I'm so proud of my boys because when I helped in their classes, and the perceived "left behind" would run to hug me. This one adorable kid cried out, "Oh man, I love your son, he is my best friend, he is my only friend." The surprising part about that, most kids pulled me aside to say that. So tell me again, can you make a difference in the people's lives in our world? Look around your house, start there.

Really think about that. We will never know the affect we have on the world do we? Sometimes I wonder if that is where people get bored because they aren't acknowledged for what they do well. I make a difference in this world and I believe God has given me more when He sees how I do at home with my boys. I get to raise two boys that will love the unloved. I will NEVER know by doing that, that a massacre was stopped because my love, put into my boys, transferred a lonely kid out of a life of anger. I've heard of stories of people considering suicide made a pact with themselves to walk down the street saying that if one person smiled then they wouldn't kill themselves. Umm, that is scary truly because honestly, I have some doubts on that happening. I'm not sure people look at me when I have an air of depression and sadness. Why do we look away?

My heart burst yesterday because I know what I am called to do. Every time I see a lost teen, my heart breaks. My calling is to step into the lives of teens. I am in my calling for sure, and I know there is way more coming. My job right now is to use my resources to breathe life into others. We can't take away what just happened. We can choose to make a positive difference and stand in our strength in the Lord. I can't tell you how much you affect lives just with what you choose to do with this massacre. The shooting in our church and the failures of our pastor TOOK OUT at least 1,000 people in their walk with the Lord. Seriously, having faith or your identity in people is DEADLY. When they fail, you are completely lost and with out God in your heart. I beg you to lift your eyes up, where your ONLY help comes from, and walk through your questions and anger with Him. I beg you to not be taken out. Take a stand that you are NOT going to be a huge "take" in loss.

We need Christians to be the strongest voice in a situation like this. So many times I see Christians lay down and die with, justifying the lack of movement in their lives. More challenges are to come, that is written. What are you going to do in adversity? You got this, and we need you. Speak into someone's life today. Mend relationships that are strained as you don't know how much time you have with them. Love on someone. Protect the innocence of your children. Teach them what a Godly response is to a heart breaking devastation. Teach them to rise up to adversity and fight for their lives. Teach them to not be a "take on society" but a voice.

Thank you God for giving me the strength to choose to love in my own loss. My boys have watched me for the last couple of years fumble through my divorce and take the higher road, the road less traveled. This is a must for my boys and I will not create anything less than the best possible. It kills my flesh and selfish angry ways, and it is worth it to me to affect my boys in a profound way through this trial of divorce. They will see anger and tears, but mostly they will see I can only do this with God. They will see HIS LOVE.

The greatest love is when it is toward the betrayer. If given the chance, would I turn and hug the shooter? Would I stand up and walk toward him as he sandblasted me with bullets just so I could tell him he is loved? Would I crumble with him to the ground and not release until his body stopped fighting and he owned that he was loved? Would I pray over him, forgive him and stand by him as he struggled with God? I can honestly answer YES to that in my own life with my betrayers. To be able to do that is truly humbling and something God set in me because I ASKED for it. He has answered my prayers.

I dare you to move..........I dare you to stand up

You are doing great, keep Going, -Amanda

1. Listen to <u>Praise You in this Storm</u> by Casting Crowns.

2. Listen to <u>Dare you to move</u> by Switchfoot.

3. Speak into 10 lives today.

4. Mend 4 strained relationships this week.

5. Pick 2 teens that you can encourage weekly.

6. Journal about the experience you created with speaking into others lives and mending strained relationships.

7. Create that again for a week until you feel completely clear in your relationships.

8. When a tragic loss is in your area, what are some things that you can do to provide love and support to the community?

9. If you have children, what attitude are you passing down to them around loss?

Journal

Insight • Answers • Downloads
AHA's • Wisdom • Findings

Unleash Your LAUGHTER

CRACK DOESN'T KILL, IT MAKES YOU LAUGH

In interest of protecting my friend's pride, I will rename her Carey. Carey and I have known each other since college. We really became friends when we signed up for the summer backpacking trip through the Grand Canyon, rim to rim. When you camp and hang in a van for fourteen days, you are going to either never talk again, or be bonded for life. This trip was for sure one of our best. It ignited a fire in us to see more places. So we did.

She graduated before me and started working as a flight attendant. For my graduation present she got us open ended tickets to Alaska. We left after I graduated which proved to be fantastic and quite the adventure. When it is only the two of you, before "selfies," were popular, you just take pictures of each other at different places. We got incredibly bored with that and decided to start doing "crack shots." This by far created a humor addiction for not only this trip, but many years after that. The idea was to get an interesting back-ground with one of us in there, along with a tad of crack. To get these with people around, or just the two of us, brought so much laughter, that we often peed our pants a little.

Here are some of our best shots so far.

Since I am a scrap-booker, I covered up my crack, but not Carey's. I think it is because it is that awesome of an art piece. Carey still holds the 1st place ribbon for the best crack shot pose. On my 40th birthday trip to Mexico we had the enrollment gift down with a stranger on our yacht. Odd? Inappropriate? Well, all I have to say to that is I have some of the best memories ever.

I urge you to up your "fun factor" with your kids, spouse and friends. Yes, the Alaska trip was incredible, but honestly the only parts of the trip I remember are the crack shots. The photos remind me of all the great things we saw, but the laughter makes the memories last forever.

People have asked me what my book is about. My book is about liberating you into joy and freedom to laugh at your life, circumstances and the journey (good and bad). It is to dig in deep and also laugh until you cry. I love going up to a stranger and dancing with them. The laughter and shock is so incredible. I love finding "funny" in everything I'm experiencing and usually enjoy the people around me joining in with belly laughter. If I make someone laugh, then that was a great day.

I have gotten feedback from friends that this bugs them that I treat myself that way. What way? Completely surrender to "my pride" and "looking good program" and giving the gift of life for ten minutes? Take a look at why it bugs you? Maybe your desire to be "put together" all the time is way deeper than that. How much have you missed out on in life because you cared what people thought or you felt judged? I definitely know when I am in dripping death sarcasm, and I also know when I am in my gift. What's your gift? Are you using it? What is the opposite of your gift? For example my gifts are influence, quick wit, encouragement, laughter and joy. The opposite of that, the counterfeit is sarcasm which is unexpressed anger usually. It usually ends in both parties feeling drained instead of filled up.

The world needs you and your gifts!

Your fear of not being liked or embarrassed is a total "take" from the people around you. I like to call that a brown vote. If you know what I mean. Crap.

FUN FACTOR IDEAS

1. How and where can you add fun into your life?
2. Ask family/friends how FUN you are to be around (scale of 1-10)
3. Think of a series of pictures you can create with your friends or family that will bring you much joy, laughter and memories. Example: Planking on weird items & Crack shots
4. When was the last time you had a surrendered "belly laugh?"
5. Are you a fun person to be around? If not, can you give in that area and try something new?
6. Life is too serious, go out and create ten fun experiences.

Email me about them at sharpdesignsinc@mac.com

Journal
Insight • Answers • Downloads
AHA's • Wisdom • Findings

Journal
Insight • Answers • Downloads
AHA's • Wisdom • Findings

TRUTH IS......I MISS YOU

I know, I know you are going into all sorts of meaning on this title. Guess what? I have no idea what I'm going to write about AND I HAVE AN AMAZING AHA AT THE END I PROMISE. What God writes in between is up to Him. I would love to take you on a full journey. I hope you have a few minutes to spare? I believe you will get something really neat at the end. So here we go, find and play "Warning Sign" by Coldplay and see what comes up around this song. Songs bring us memories and emotions of all kinds. I want you to think about what comes up for YOU during this song, not what the songwriter meant by the song. PAUSE. BREATHE. GO TO YOUR HEART, THAT PLACE THAT HAS A VOID. WHAT IS THE VOID?

I miss you, in this moment means....LOSS. All kinds, mine and those I love. The relationships that have shifted to fleeting thoughts, the dad that never chose to connect, the husband that coiled inward and was lost, watching a friend make extremely hurtful choices to others, a friend grieving over the idea of not even knowing what she enjoys anymore, a marriage that leaves her feeling "never enough," giving your life to something and no recognition in the end, a womb not inviting in a baby, an amazing man with the faith of a mountain still in pain from cancer, a family torn on the loss of how their baby girl was before a drowning accident, friends that have given everything they have got and then their house floods, my friend grieving the dad he never met and the grand father he just lost, the woman a friend believed to be "the one" and ending in great disappointment, and finally the news of a husband dying in a tragic motorcycle accident.

I was asked last night how I do it? How I do what? How have you made it through this divorce and are still hopeful? Well, I feel like this would be powerful enough to write down in my "journal," my book. I've never done this but I want you to listen to this song again. THIS TIME IN THE BACKGROUND AS YOU KEEP READING. The truth is...... I miss you, means to me, I MISS ME. I MISS GOD AND SITTING IN HIS LAP. I miss all the things that used to make me smile and laugh, the people that created that with me, I miss sitting in the Father's lap and nakedly baring it all. All emotions, bringing it to Him. When I look at all this swirling around me, there is a lot of LOSS, great LOSS. Everyone has it, and everyone is coping or not coping with it. My answer to "how do you do it," is this....I CRAWL BACK INTO HIS OPEN ARMS. That's it. It's that simple.

I have spent so many days in the fetal position with a heavy heart for all these burdens and brokenness. All the loss around me actually ends up coming to a root of all of my personal loss and where I am in the healing process with it. I take it back to HIM. It is an amazing place to be truly. You don't have to be FIXED up to get in his lap. You can be the equivalent to the used woman in the street grasping at his feet, looking up and seeing that warm, gentle smile of forgiveness and acceptance. It is a choice for me daily, I really want you to get that. I choose to bring it to Him or I choose to go down a death spiral of pain. I choose to love on those around me that accept my love, and then I choose to go back to Him and get refueled with HIS energy. I want to be a "give" to this world, not a "take."

The only way I can do that is if I am giving from a full cup, not a broken leaking one. I want to have "fruit" that lasts with people, not tossed out with the next opinion. I want them to remember how I made them feel instead of what I said.

When you are in the struggle, people have no idea where you are at unless you tell them. You have to make the move for support and help. You have to be personally responsible and pro-active and willing to shift. If you can step back and think about all the loss WE ALL are experiencing then maybe you'll understand why no one is asking you "what's wrong?" There is a lot of demolished, empty, cracked china sitting around giving from nothing.

THE LIFE GIVING KEYS TO MAKING IT THROUGH PAIN FOR ME HAS BEEN A BLANKET OF THINGS.

Crawling in HIS lap THROUGH EVERY EMOTION. Not just the defeated exhausted ones. I mean the screaming at the top of your lungs when no one is home. He's had all emotions and can most certainly take yours. I think it is insulting to only bring broken Amanda to him.

CAUSE THE TRUTH IS.....HE MISSES YOU.

Inner circle of ONLY positive friends around me through healing. This is KEY, downward spirals are a given with negative friends.

CAUSE THE TRUTH IS... THEY MISS YOU AND WANT TO SUPPORT YOU.

People committed to praying for me, visualizing and believing for my breakthrough

CAUSE THE TRUTH IS...THEY MISS HEARING YOUR VICTORIES.

Dive in to studies and books that are highly suggested about moving through pain and loss with God. I have many that rocked my world.

CAUSE THE TRUTH IS....HE MISSES YOU TEACHING YOU.

DREAM!! I use genesisdreamboard.com. If you don't have dreams, why even get out of bed, seriously? I sat with a friend last night and the change in her heart in an hour of talking about what did she use to love to do. She is committed to dream and show me. It was a blast to see the sparkle in her eyes again. I love that woman and know she's going to pull out of the heaviness.

CAUSE THE TRUTH IS...THEY MISS YOU AND THAT SPARKLE IN YOUR EYES.

An action plan of what you want, and hardcore accountability. By the way, Accountability is NOT you waiting for someone to check in with you. Accountability is YOU TAKING ON YOUR LIFE and having that persons face in your mind that wants to know what you created. It's me saying "I want this to happen, and making it happen because I can't wait to celebrate with that person."

CAUSE THE TRUTH IS....WE MISS YOU TAKING ON YOUR LIFE INSTEAD OF EXPECTING US TO.

Gratitude! When you are in a high place spew gratitude and thankfulness for your freedom, your friendships and how people and God have effected you. You can always tell when I am in a great place because my Face Book page is exploding with Love for people. If you are down, then do the same thing. This will refuel you big time.

CAUSE THE TRUTH IS....WE MISS YOUR GRATITUDE AND NOTICING THAT WE MATTER TO YOU.

No addictions! No addictions, means it all. We all have a vice that is "our button" that is easily pushed. Is it drugs, alcohol, gossip, sad movies, eating poorly, exercising too much, negative self talk for you?

CAUSE THE TRUTH IS....WE ALL SEE IT AND WE ALL MISS THE REAL YOU.

Having a huge WHY behind your action. It has got to be so important to you that you would run into traffic to go get that dream out. Basically, my latest goal set was to have 100 connections with my boys of their choosing. The WHY isn't so I can feel like a great mom. The WHY is because my boys deserve to have me in their lives. I was gifted with them, and I don't have a ton of time with them. They deserve to have my FULL attention and LOVE for a couple hours a day. I choose to put my phone in my room from 2:30-7pm while they are home from school. This has taken away so much frustration, as they were always interrupting my "important" work on my phone and computer. The feedback from them for the first three nights was gut wrenching. "Mom I really love to be able to talk to you now that your phone is away, thank you so much for doing that for me. That means a lot."

CAUSE THE TRUTH IS....WE MISS YOU MOMMY.

THE MOST IMPORTANT THING!!! DON'T PLAY GOD. DON'T PLAY GOD means NO ONE ON THIS EARTH IS YOUR RESPONSIBILITY. You are responsible for YOU and YOU ONLY. Did you just feel that? Seriously, the friggin HUGE yoke that was self built on your back just dropped off. Can you even accept this last thing? I AM NOT GOD, I DON'T HAVE YOUR ANSWERS, HE DOES. I DON'T KNOW WHAT HE IS TEACHING YOU BUT I CAN ENCOURAGE YOU AND I CAN LOOK INTO THE MIRROR AND SAY GOD WHY DO I HAVE EMOTION AROUND ALL THIS LOSS I HEAR ABOUT. He always takes me to my own personal loss and the open, festering flesh wound there and we walk through it.

Really, when I am wallowing in my emotions around some perceived loss, it comes down to this, I miss God. I miss who I was before allowing loss to steal from me, and who I truly want to be. THE ROOT IS ME AND ME IS ALL I CAN CHANGE.

CAUSE THE TRUTH IS........I MISS YOU! I hope that this brings great freedom!!! All you got is YOU and HIM truly. Find peace in that, and you are on your way to recovery from the worlds onslaught. Feel LOVELY again!

Action • Growth • Awareness

1. Listen to <u>Warning Sign</u> by Coldplay again. What is the void for you?

2. Listen to <u>Lovely</u> by Sara Haze

3. What did you get from this today? What is God telling you? How are you coping with your losses? Who is missing out on you because of what you've chosen.

4. Create 3 fun outings of connection for the next week and really share from a vulnerable place what their friendship means to you. If not in the same state, make sure it is a media where you can see their face in front of you and their emotions.

5. Create a dream board with words and pictures of your desires.

6. Buy and Read at some point <u>Life's Healing Choices: Freedom from Hurts, Hang-ups and Habits</u> by John Baker

7. What do you believe to be your addictions (void fillers) when you are in a dark space?

Journal
Insight • Answers • Downloads
AHA's • Wisdom • Findings

Journal

Insight • Answers • Downloads
AHA's • Wisdom • Findings

MOVEMBER

Have you noticed how many funny stories and pictures there are on social media? So much material for a comedian, so little time. Since I have a passion to laugh about pretty much everything, this often brings a ton of joy. Just like the dating sites, I was motivated to poke fun of all the beard pictures that are loaded on Face Book in November. Movember is the month that a lot of men choose into not shaving their facial hair. It started out with the mustache and now has grown into the whole face being overgrown. I believe men felt left out in some way around the marketing of breast cancer awareness. We are all clear men are protective of their "parts" and now they have an awareness month to find a cure for cancer down there.

It is funny to me that we just state it as Breast Cancer Awareness month and pass out bumper stickers that say "save the tatas" and "I love boobs," or "boobs can use your support." Or my favorite, "big or small, lets save them all." Now that I think about it though, their bumper stickers would be "I love ball sacks," "save the nuts," "nuts can use your support," or it would be weird to say "big or small, lets save them all." I'm sorry, but do you see the problem here? No woman is going to buy that bumper sticker to put it on their car. If you do see one on their car about men, it would probably be more like, "I love to kick nuts," or "I'm a ball buster."

This is probably why they decided against bumper sticker campaigns and went with something they know how to do really well. Facial Hair. It's almost like you can feel all men "coming together" in November in a secret society. When they see a bearded stranger in the grocery store they do a cool head nod or a high five. Instantly they have bonded........through a beard. Any comments fuel them to do less trimming and actually take the time to use a brush to frizz it completely to its full potential.

Honestly, for me, it is a great "diet" month. As I stare at the monstrosity of pure laziness all around me. The scraggly beards growing over their lips, food chunks and dried boogers encrusted and embedded within. It in fact creates a space where I'm really just not that hungry. That is called a win win. The part that bugs me the most is that they can't stand when we grow one in our 80's. It's hypocritical really.

After a week of this madness on Facebook, I decided to join in on the support of the cure.

CALLED TO LOVE....A TRUE GIFT

When you experience resistance and excuses to something you are going through, that its probably an indication of some treasure at the end. I personally can't write until I am out of judgment, anger and a WWF wrestling match with Him on the topic. Then and only then, is the AHA revealed. If I can be an instrument that supplies quality fruit today then that humbles me to no end.

I have found by being a "people watcher" my whole life, that blaring and shocking commonalities cock my head to the side in question. When offended, I get to step back and say "I wonder what it is in that person that is creating this response in me?" Well, if I'm ready to work on a subject, then God gives me HUGE experiences to practice and falter through. Always, always impurities rise to the top. **It is important to understand the enemy wants you to stay as a scared child in the corner regretting your ugliness, because being hopeless is a snare that disables for life. God didn't call us to be perfect. He called us to Love. That's it. Love ourselves and each other.** Based on a snapshot of the world, how are we doing? To say I have been tested in the subject of LOVE is an understatement. His love and the enemies plan of counterfeit love can be intertwined.

Recently, I was in so much confusion (not of God), fear (not of God) and cried out to God for an answer in scripture. I was thrilled to have this scripture to gauge how I am doing on the topic of love. When in relationship with others, He showed me, instead of taking things personal, use this gauge of love. Once you know where you are at, you can shift. Once you know where others are at, you can remove yourself from the abuse and pray. The reason I do this, is that scripture is ultimate truth, therefore can not be manipulated by the enemy.

Love is patient, love is kind. It does not envy, it does not boast, it is not proud. It does not dishonor others, it is not self-seeking, it is not easily angered, it keeps no record of wrongs. Love does not delight in evil but rejoices with the truth. It always protects, always trusts, always hopes, always perseveres. – 1 Corinthians 13:4-6

Even though I have heard this scripture read at many weddings, including mine, I had not really listened to the words. I have no clue how to LOVE. Without Him I am hopelessly NOT capable of grasping even a percentage of LOVE. So with that being said, you can see all around you, counterfeit, selfish, devouring, enemy infiltrated and manipulated love. It is everywhere. What people do in the name of LOVE is truly appalling. It's as if we should all be named Judas, and Judas the 2nd. What I do in the name of LOVE is disgusting. **Masking opinions, feedback, hurtful rumors, the need to be right, or my own pain under the umbrella of LOVE is demolishing to all those around me.** Now that the mirror has been turned on me I get to choose personal responsibility instead of pointing the finger at someone else to change. "Stop playing God Amanda, HE speaks to you, why don't you think HE can speak to them?" was given to me as truth as I was discussing with my friend.

Have you ever met someone that everyone seems to love, they profess great love for others, they are "moving mountains," they give to the poor and support great causes, and appears to be loving, yet when the testing fire comes, you see things that burn your eyes, ears and heart? **Have I been this person to people? Yes probably so.** Now, instead of getting "sucked in" to that space, I can stand back and pray. When I feel people move out of my space, I can quickly shift the attitude I have, and gauge where I am in love.

To be patient, kind, not envy or boast, to not be proud but humble, not dishonor or embarrass people, not be self seeking and step on others to get to "the top," not keep a record of wrongs or delight in evil happening to others. Be excited about truth, always protect, hope and persevere. What more can we ask for? That should keep us all busy for a lifetime.

I have been so confused in some past relationships as to why they were so difficult. Why actions and the words spoken over me did not leave me feeling good. This scripture I got was perfect. It was such a relief to have this to gauge where people are at with me. Now I can look at their fruit in a non-judgmental way, and say "this person is lacking love for me." It was so life giving to me and I was able to pluck out the deathly daggers, and move into a space of prayer. Now that that was done, God had even more for me. Usually, when you judge someone or something, it is a quality you dislike about yourself.

I was in a situation with my ex that brought out a side of me that transferred all the anger I had bottled up for weeks. He was the lucky recipient. I stopped halfway at least, and said "let's stick to the facts because I obviously have emotion coming up that has nothing to do with you." Progress? Yes. More to look at? Yes. I woke up the next morning, and used the LOVE gauge on myself, around Him. I got it, I'm disgusted by the qualities that I spoke to him out of my pain. I literally repeated what had been done to me several times. Look whose judging now?

I was humbled to say the least. I chose to quickly apologize and move myself out of shame of my actions. It is important to understand that my actions are putting me in decay (jail), not theirs. I am called to love period. **In fact, God isn't much impressed with us loving the ones that brag on us, verbally rain down glory on us and fill our egos with satisfaction of our awesome selves. HE LOOKS at the fruit that we have with the people that are extremely hurtful, unloving, rude, obnoxious and hateful.**

Have you ever thought that maybe your purpose was to just LOVE? LOVE no matter what? It seems that is the most challenging purpose of them all. Do any of us really have LOVE down? What now? Well, I can only control what I do in life. I literally can not play God and move anyone to realize their actions toward me. So instead of living a life of frustration, I choose to let God take care of it. This has brought me much freedom and He does a way better job than I do. I chose to apologize and discuss my hurtful demeaning words. If there is one thing I have learned with freedom, I have to keep short accounts with people. I have always loved the theory of beating someone to the apology. If they are open to hearing it, I will share it. If I am unaware, I hope that I have created the space for them to openly check in with me. I don't want to live a life of being un-teachable, closed, and un-loving. I want to live a life filled with God's love, and have it be full of amazing friendships and memories.

I want the experience of ME to be HIS love through me. Not perfection, but loving grace that allows you and I to make mistakes, and the space to correct them.

Action • Growth • Awareness

1. Listen to <u>Mighty Breath of God</u> by Jesus Culture

2. Set aside 30 minutes & Listen to <u>Garden</u> by Misty Edwards

   I want to share a song with you that has brought me quickly into a space with God for him to download. I love it and it deeply moves me. If you have a moment, play the song and ask God to reveal to you what he wants. I dare you to be more excellent than you are.

3. Where in life can you be a more loving person and with whom?

4. Where are you at with loving people? Where are you at with loving yourself? I have heard it said you are only capable of giving love to the capacity that you are able to receive love.

5. Write out the words in the scripture and grade yourself on where you are at with people that are HARD to love for you. Dig deep and find the root of why?

6. Buy & Read at some point - Crossroads by William Paul Young

Journal

Insight • Answers • Downloads
AHA's • Wisdom • Findings

Journal

Insight • Answers • Downloads
AHA's • Wisdom • Findings

Unleash Your LAUGHTER

For 12 days near Christmas,
the dating site offered me

12 wearing mullets
11 men with piercings
10 bow ties (only)
9 bathroom shots
8 boys a lying
6 men a posing
5 golden teeth
4 calling me
3 on parole
2 married men
and a guy that was seventy three

JUST PRAY AND BE A LIGHT

Well, I'm saddened again by yet another teen school shooting. There is so much on Facebook about remembering these beautiful children that were killed at Sandy Hook. It grieves this mom to the soul. Loss, like I've said before, brings up all our own personal loss. Along with fear, anger, and every emotion possible. While on a call, we closed in prayer and God brought an idea to me I've never pondered. "Amanda pray for those teens that are struggling right now mentally and emotionally. Pray against the enemy's plan to use them as puppets for the next event." This was eye opening so I did. It brought up so much emotion in me as I prayed.

This is the core of what I believe, we are called to love and that's it. If you only have the power to just reach your children, isn't that enough? I didn't think it was until now. I have the authority to pray over my boys and speak life giving words to them. I catch myself daily, being overcritical and opinionated on what they are doing or not doing. I have the opportunity to build confidence, laughter and amazing memories with them. If I don't, who will? What I do at home sets them up for who they are at school. Who they are at school and how they deal with the pressures of life such as bullying, follows them into their young adult life and so on. I can make a huge impact just by being an incredible mom. My boys, just like me will affect thousands of people. The question is how will they affect them?

I posted this on Facebook after the shooting and it is got so much response in just an hour I felt like that was confirmation to keep writing on this subject.

Just want to put my prayer request out there that any struggling youth swayed by darkness seek help in order to get healthy again, that we compassionately start noticing and helping kids that are crying out and creating negative attention. Lord I just pray that any desires in this world to one up the last tragedy are silenced in those hearts. We can all do our part by being loving to those within our reach, and by opening our eyes to the internally afflicted youth crying to be "seen." If you are unable to love on your teens, then find a friend to help. It takes a village to raise an idiot and a community to raise a leader. -Amanda

Here's the kicker - I can and will do more. I know I am called to breathe life into people, bridge the gap between what's true about them and their disbelief. Go out there and find a group of kids and create something with them. Move them forward in their lives. Be their surrogate parent. Fill in the gaps where their parents are exhausted. Help anyone. I am grieved for all the kids pondering getting negative attention in this horrific way. What about all the suicides happening every minute. Instead of becoming overwhelmed and being beaten like them, light a torch in your heart and reach out. They are everywhere. Can we all open our eyes and start noticing the heart wrenching cries of desperation in these teens. We grasp on to tragedy and let it carry us down into the pit. Make a stand to love like none other, be a light and pray.

I had the pleasure and privilege to see Nick Vujcich in person. I brought my boys so they could hear and never forget to keep going. Here is this man that was born without arms and legs and has changed millions of lives with his story. His story of not giving up is unforgettable. Can you imagine not only overcoming "the lack" in his life to becoming a speaker to millions? It had me in tears to watch my boys stare at him in wonder not judgment. You could see it in their eyes that they "got it" that night. Stop sulking and find something, anything that would make a positive impact on your world, you reach. Stop comparing your gifts to others. I have always told myself I'm a crappy writer and then I decided to start writing. It's funny because at first I cared about my grammar and run on sentences and now I got it. "Be a light" in whatever format you can. If we all change the expression on one person's face a day, that is a lot of transformation. Right before I finished this book, I read in the Circle maker, "are you called to write? Then do it out of obedience to God not caring if anyone reads it." That was the final motivating word for me.

Action • Growth • Awareness

1. Watch any & all Nick Vujcich videos

2. Buy and read at some point the Circle Maker by Mark Batterson

3. Listen to <u>I Won't Give Up</u> by Jason Mraz

4. Listen to <u>Breathe Me</u> by Sia

Journal
Insight • Answers • Downloads
AHA's • Wisdom • Findings

#raisingcomedians

One of the ways I get past the mediocre days in life is to just stop, drop and roll with life. Since I am a photographer, I am sensitive to possible subjects, especially for comedy. I have taught my boys to look for this as well. Some of our best memories have been spur of the moment shots while out and about. I encourage you to try this. Why? Well, it brings your fun side out, it cures boredom, and creates a lot of memories with your friends and family. My boys are still young and not easily embarrassed. Here are some examples of the hundreds I have created for Facebook entertainment. If you are a drag to be around, then you will attract drags. I can say this because I lost my laughter in the midst of my pain at one point. Now I laugh through and during the healing. These are some of the ways I keep it real in my family.

I picked these pictures because I want you to understand that there was opportunity for me to choose out of fun completely. The first one was at the zoo and it was hot and I was exhausted after traveling. I pushed myself to connect with my boys. They did crazy pictures and I did so did I. The mushroom looked so phallic to me that I couldn't stop laughing. They wanted me to hang off of something for a picture so I did. I'm clear those are my issues AND it created so much joy in all of us to just laugh and laugh with each other. No, I didn't share my thoughts on the mushroom with the boys.

The 2nd one, my boys and I just got done at a movie and they were expressing how much they miss their dad. "Well, let's call him, but after I plank Mr. Peanut." Why? It creates a space of just plain dumb laughter, the side splitting kind because I am teaching my boys to not be concerned with others opinions on them. Me getting on top of that metal statue was hilarious and totally worth the crowd shaking their heads as a seven year old learned to use my Iphone camera.

The third is my dentist. This poor guy had the pleasure of fixing a tooth that despite 5 shots, my gum was not numb. Can you imagine knowing you are hurting someone and trying to drill their tooth out? Instead of going into flat out tears of pain, I decided to take my phone and take a picture of him from the angle I saw him for 2 hours. We all laughed and we both relaxed and completed the task with uplifted spirits. I could have chosen, I will never do that again and be toothless.

I hope this encourages you to look at life from a different stand point and challenge you to choose joy in the storm. Smile at what the fan is slinging in your face. We can't stop all circumstances but we can stop our response to them.

If you are seriously humor challenged, hang out with fun people. You become who you hang around I hear. If you are coming from a place of needing to be right that fun isn't for you. How is that working for you?

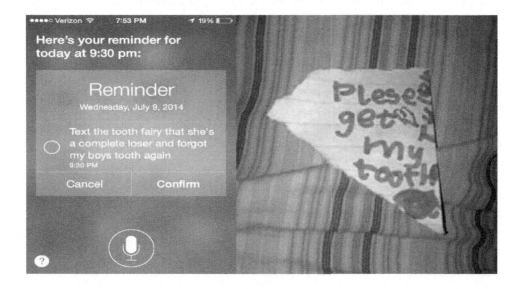

"What a nag, I said I'd do it 3 days ago." This evening we laughed so hard cause I made this message in his room while saying good night. I walked back in my room and his note was on my bed. It was so funny because he knows it's me and we just keep pretending. His belly laughter with my reminder to SIRI was so much fun.

IF YOU SAY GO... I WILL GO.

I have been pondering how, when and what to write from a recent experience I created. After losing the whole piece two times, I decided this one must need to be written. Weird? Yes. Stopping me? No. I will take that as a sign that either that was written by me (crap), or that it was such a needed message I should ask for it again. Either way, I'm writing.

So I had quite the challenge before me as my boys drove off with their dad over the Christmas holidays. Nothing worse than releasing your children to go make memories and not be a part of any of them. As I stood looking out the window, a rush of fear came over me, all the things that could go wrong. Well, even if I was in the car, could I really stop that from happening? Instead of sulking and being a needy drainer over the holidays, I decided to ask God what I might do instead. Ten days to myself is a long time when you are use to being needed every hour of the day.

I have to say, I've been really struggling about our ranch project still not happening. We are moving forward and yet still don't have much to show for it. I believe it is still my calling and yet what do I do in the meantime? I guess I could be a dreamless woman aimlessly latching on to others dreams to feel adequate about myself and what I'm doing with my time. Or I could just ask "what do you have for me today Lord?" I feel like He answered "why don't you go hang out with people that are suffering like you?" What? "Can you think of anyone that might feel lonely?" "No, everyone is with family." Oh? Seriously? Yes.

The blanket project was born quickly and grew over night. Honestly, if you feel that God might be in it, MOVE! I immediately had all the ideas downloaded on how to accomplish the task. He laid it on hearts to give through my announcement on Face Book. $670 was raised in 3 days by a handful of donors. My sister wanted to help and so did my mom. Then I got the idea of honoring the little precious kids shot in the school shooting. This turned into a 26 random acts of kindness. As days went by, 2 friends of mine whom have lost loved ones this year, came to mind. 28 blankets wrapping the homeless in warmth in remembrance to the lost. Done.

What I experienced was gut wrenching as all these people could have been me. I was looking into the eyes that were made of mirrors. It was an un-settling awareness that one choice could bring me poverty. These were all people just like me. They wanted to "be seen," be important to someone, anyone, be loved. These beloved people did not look away in shame. They pierced you with their eyes, hoping you have the guts to look into theirs and feel their harmlessness. I don't have a judgment on why they are there, I have a compassion on why they believe they should stay there. I have a rage about the lies that are being believed and muffling the voice of people that God sees as his own, whether they accept him or not. Then again, if I look into those mirrored eyes, I will take a look at all of that for me. What sign am I holding up today that is a complete lie about myself?

We are all the same. We all have loss and disappointments. We have all been abandoned by someone. We have all had people quit on us. We are all screaming inside wishing that people could read our signs. What would be your heart cry to the world?

I burn with passion for youth and I don't know what to do about it? What God? What is the next step for me? Please, I beg for your direction? I am so grieved by the teens of today and all the counterfeits they are settling for. It enrages me to hear young women being used for the selfishness of man only to feel loved, even for a moment. I have a ministry and yet how do I move forward? This dream has not gone away for many years now. I am stuck in cement blocks, **I am homeless to my calling.** Well, what now? Be useless and never move? As I watched Evan Almighty, God (in the movie) said **"Want to change the world? Do 1 random act of kindness at a time."**

So that is what I will be doing until further direction. I will be doing 1 random act of kindness at a time. I will speak life in to teens, I will be a light, I will encourage, and I will wait until you say go......and then I will go. Why? Because I have enough. I do enough. I am enough.

Would love if you would find us on Facebook under Legacy Project Group, LIKE the page to stay in the loop of the future projects. If you have teens that you think would benefit from having me in their life, send me a note on Legacy's page. I would love to have an accountability group for teens on Facebook that moves them forward in leadership through their choices and then create projects that we come together and do that change their existence forever.

If you feel like you want to get behind my heart for teens, I would love ANY donations to work with. Go to our non-profit account which is currently collected through Razoo. Five years from now who knows where we will be. Hopefully on our land working with people and loving on them.

1. Listen to <u>If You Say Go I Will Go</u> by Rita Springer

2. Listen to <u>Yearn</u> by Shane & Shane. If you find a video on youtube.com that is black and white where they are holding up signs, watch that instead.

3. If you were homeless, what would your sign read.

4. What is your heart cry to the world? Your deepest pain.

5. Watch the movie <u>Evan Almighty.</u>

6. When was the last time you were in fervent prayer around the dreams you feel that God has given you?

7. Do something for a less fortunate person in your life.

Journal
Insight • Answers • Downloads
AHA's • Wisdom • Findings

Unleash Your LAUGHTER

FACEBOOK MUSINGS –
KINDA LIKE DEEP THOUGHTS BY MANDY INSTEAD OF JACK HANDY

I wonder if God does April fools jokes? I look around and see some pretty funny looking people. Oh and the naked mole rat.

The only thing better than old school 90's praise and worship would be if Ron Burgandy played his flute solo and Snoop Dogg broke it down in the background with a couple Lil Jons "yeeaaah"

I need some me time. And when I say ME, that means laying in bed all day, looking in the mirror and saying affirmations, wearing a mesh half shirt to Walmart just for fun, and massive solo dance party to really inappropriate music at level 10 with full white man's overbite and my best moves.

Seriously angry that Miley ruined the foam finger......now I feel embarrassed to wear mine.

That moment when you have to use inappropriate visuals to encourage your boys to shower more. #rashfromheretodere☐☐ #dingleberrymadness☐☐ #burningurine☐☐ #swampbutt☐☐

At least once a week you should do personal inventory and ask yourself "am I one of the people of Walmart?"

Just got a notice from Alex from eHarmony. He is looking for a thrust-worthy relationship. Do you think I am thrust-worthy?

I really put the fun in dysfunctional.

I seriously can't live another day without you. I yearn for you to play music to me. When you are in a room you command attention and that makes you hotter than anything. Cowbell, you and me together would make beautiful music.

Does everyone know Christmas is not about celebrating the chance to tell your dreams and desires to an Oreo eating, heavy breathing, sweating old man with rope tied on beard. And Easter ain't about a basket filled to the brim with sugar and half melted Easter bunnies, loose dirty jelly beans held in a child's germ filled hand. It is about this special guy I know well, laugh often with and get answers to my next move and much help on how to raise my boys. It's about family coming together and re connecting. It's about your kids laughing as they search for plastic eggs and the surprise gift that they've requested. It's about memories and love. Have an amazingly connected Easter!

Should I do parkour? I can fall down a mean set of stairs.

HIDING UNDER A ROCK
OR STANDING ON "THE ROCK"

Both actually, thanks for asking. It's funny because right after I declared that I was going to finally write the book I've been sitting on for ten years, all of a sudden I'm disinterested in being open for God to write through me, until today. I have not known how to write on the reoccurring event happening in my life...death.

I have been standing on "the rock" most definitely as it's the only way I could have made it through the last year. The grieving process around a death is quite like a train derailment. Some cars smashed out of shape to be unrecognizable and others are completely unharmed. So are the rooms in my heart. Some completely bolted shut with sharp twisted metal soldered to an iron clad door and some so open to healing that mending begins immediately. In fact, not affected emotionally at all. It really depends on how much cleaning I've done or allowed in each room.

In a years time, 8 people I have had relationship with or family members have passed away. All different ways of passing and all completely different grieving processes. The process depended on how close I was to them, was it sudden or a long illness, complete shock or expected at some point. Did they leave an amazing legacy or a pattern of relationships that weren't cherished. Then the hardest part for me was it was: so much loss at once I couldn't compartmentalize what emotion I was having and who it was directed toward. Whom was I grieving and was I angry or sad?

Bottom line, when loss happens around us, it puts a microscope on our own personal loss and where we are at with it. For me with my losses, I have finally come to the end of myself, and allowed God to come in and take over the control room. To do that I must surrender to the fact that I can not do it without him. This has been the greatest gift to me because, when you come from that place, there is little resistance or fear. This is when I started experiencing the best love, grace, surrender, joy acceptance and extreme contentment. When I give up the need to fix my life and find solutions to my loss that is when abundance ushers itself in.

Nothing has turned out the way I had planned, nothing. I certainly can't control when people die and I totally CAN control how it affects me and how I act. My biggest struggle has been watching those left behind hurting. I do also realize that if I'm going to play a bigger game and meet 50-100 people a month and connect to their hearts, this ups the odds of experiencing pain in life. That fear is certainly not going to keep me from reaching out. I asked God what He wanted me to do or be, I feel He said "just love on whomever you can." So that is what I've done, and in that giving of love, I have received truckloads back. That has created a space of joyful contentment that is undeniable to those who know me. In my humanness, I even questioned "Am I numb Lord and unaffected?" "Am I heartless and unemotional now?" "No my child you are so filled up and pliable that you can be used to support others in their pain, which creates healing in you."

This is life altering. This is what I've prayed for, I am humbled. This brings up a some great questions…..

Are you a safe haven, approachable for others to trust you?

Are you so broken, that people don't want to share their story, afraid it may be the tipping point into a further downward spiral?

Are you so angry that people are truly afraid of you?

Where in your life are you allowing death to prevail?

Do you stand in front of the mirror and loathe the physical side of you?

Does anyone around you know you are dying inside?

If today was your last day would the legacy left here on earth be of love and acceptance?

One thing is certain, if you open yourself to love, and journey with many people through life, the tragedy and sorrow goes way up. Journeying alone has no value to me.

I hope this encourages you to step out from under the rock and stand on "the rock." Pain is inevitable. It's up to you on how it affects you and what you do with it. I beg you to not crawl in the grave with your loss but to live big. Be love, be life.

Dedicated to some amazing, loving people in my life that have left this earth in the last year.

Action • Growth • Awareness

1. Listen to <u>If Today Was Your Last Day</u> and journal about the questions above.

Journal

Insight • Answers • Downloads
AHA's • Wisdom • Findings

SMALL **TALL** *tales*

TAKE ME DOWN TO THE PARADISE CITY

Recently, I have been working as a photographer for a company that facilitates seminars of personal growth and development. It is a blast to hang out with people that want to create a better life for themselves. I have found great value attending the 4 seminars and received life changing clarity around the ranch dream. The support I have received and tools to build confidence in my business, eventually ended up with me being the staff contract photographer. A huge thank you to all of you that encouraged me and held me accountable to what I said I wanted. It is priceless.

At one of the gigs, I had an opportunity to "have fun" and also present the photo packages I offer. I shared with them that one of my goals was to be on American Idol and yet I was so fearful that maybe my voice was awful and would sound like the people on the auditions. No one ever told me it was, I think its good, but what if I am tone deaf? I enrolled them in allowing me to sing this special song. This was a song that was extremely dear to my heart and I want played at my funeral. The audience was primed and emotionally invested with the sighs of "I had no idea that was her dream." They clapped and cheered for me to attempt the song in front of them.

I turned around and with a big nervous sigh took a moment of silence for dramatic effect. I belted out my favorite rendition of "Paradise City." I used every voice tone I could muster, I used body movements, and stretched and contorted my face. I put everything I had into this song. So much that the audience was listening and watching in a supportive fashion. They were enrolled big time.

I completed my song and started laughing hysterically and finished with something like, thank you so much for supporting me and now I'll tell you about my real gifts, my day job if you will. The stunned, confused faces of the people who didn't know me, was hilarious. The moral to this story is don't be so serious, don't be entrenched in people's opinions of you, don't be disabled by life. Have more fun!!! The adrenaline rush is massive and fantastic. I still get asked to sing that song. Make memories with people and laugh so hard you pee your pants.

WHAT DOES A HYPOCRITE WRITE ABOUT?

Where have I been lately? Hmmm. I've been grounded and content and also swirling in the worlds activity, dancing with hypocrisy and stunted in my speech. I have pondered for months how the enemy steals from me, and eventually you, if I choose to put off my writing. I believe God speaks to me when I sit down and write. I've known this since I was a little girl. A couple of months ago I thought, what in the world would I write about, I've mastered nothing. I think that is the point, sobering but true. He just wants an able body to put their fingers to the keyboard and surrender to the flow. Not a "know it all" to tell the world what they should think, but a hypocrite that is humbled daily by how God loves her. So here I am, heart connected and open with nimble fingers typing, surrendered to the voice within.

So let's dig in. Why am I a hypocrite? I make judgments about where people are at with God. I judge their faith, I judge their actions and motives, I judge it all. Everything I judge, allows an opportunity for me to be judged, everything. I even judge great things like, the contentment in the life I have (finally). I say finally but then immediately, I judge that I shouldn't feel contentment when there is massive pain and anguish going on all around me. It's as if I am grounded but also in the eye of the tornado, while looking up, unshaken by the travesty whipping large objects around and demolishing others lives. Sometimes I stick a leg out to question whether I care about people or life anymore. In the pain, I feel alive and alert again. Is this necessary? I must think so, based on results, cause I keep choosing it. I've prayed for contentment, He's given it to me, and now I'm busy trying to figure out why I am content. This is called crazy.

Surrender to your season. Bring joy to those around you in your sorrow. Love the unlovable. Forgive the perceived traitors. Pray for the ones that speak biting words behind your back. Turn the other cheek to the constant feedback of how you need to change and be more like them. Play a bigger game, whatever that is for you (not the comparison game, the "unique you" game). Flow in your gifts and set a context for life that only you can set. Be a humbled hypocrite, accept you are full of sh** (FOS) and are nothing without him. Bask in HIS greatness flowing through you. That is living in Christ for me.

God is the one that changes me. He does that the second I ask, but first I have to drop my double minded theories of what my life should look and feel like.

What has happened lately? I have gotten off the dating site. I have trusted His leading in that area. I have accepted my gifts. I have cried a thousand tears. I have befriended the lonely. I bought a FOS T-shirt and bask in the freedom it brings me. I have become a better mom and friend. I have watched love ones leave this earth. I have watched God answer my prayers and taken notice of them. I have been a hypocrite and a judge and I also see the reflection of judgment in the mirror. I have received the gift of contentment and joy for extended amounts of time. I have been provided for in ways only God could explain. This is life, this is my journey, and I wouldn't trade it for anything. Thank you for allowing this place with you, the safe haven where nakedness is accepted. Where truth can be captivating. The place I call home in my soul, my personal journal with God.

"It is not the critic who counts, not the man who points out how the strong man stumbles, or where the doer of deeds could have done them better. The credit belongs to the man in the arena, whose face is marred by dust and sweat and blood, who strives valiantly…who knows the great enthusiasms, the great devotions, who spends himself in a worthy cause, who at the best knows in the end the triumph of high achievement, and who at the worst, if he fails, at least he fails while daring greatly, so that his place shall never be with those cold and timid souls who have never known neither victory nor defeat." Teddy Roosevelt

1. Listen to <u>Oceans</u> by Hillsong

2. Listen to <u>Yearn</u> by Shane & Shane

3. Where in your life are you out of integrity?

4. What steps are you going to take to get back in to integrity with yourself and others?

5. What and whom are you judging?

6. Am I truly open to being joyful and content even in the circumstances of life?

7. How is your inner circle (people that influence you)? Pray about new people stepping into your life and possible moving others further out.

Journal

Insight • Answers • Downloads
AHA's • Wisdom • Findings

Unleash Your LAUGHTER

OR YOUR DEEPEST THOUGHTS

Below are the thoughts I could have written about, but didn't. I am putting them at the end of this book because some day I might. If I don't, I want to remember them.

How long are you going to let your counterfeit (wrong guy for me) be paraded by you, tempting you off the path? Is it about looks only, or is it about such an amazing connection that you can laugh till you cry, cry till you laugh. To be so close spiritually that it makes that person amazingly hot to you, to your soul. Not perfect and yet someone you can dig out of trenches with laughter through the pain. Someone that can't bear another day being away from you. Someone you can't pray away. Someone that finds you irreplaceable, that sees you as a gift. Someone that is connected to your dream on a heart level. The piece that just fits when you don't even know the whole puzzle. You move together in unison and build your calling easily. Once you find that person, step into courage, honor and favor. You don't need them, you want them because you challenge each other to be the best you. When wrapped in each other, there is safety. If God says yes, that is all you need. Move. That person is possibly once in a lifetime. What do you have to lose? Everything really, because you are needing to be right that you don't deserve absolute contentment in a relationship. If a person came to mind while reading this, tell them. The thoughts I sift through...........

I just woke up and realized everything I'm waiting on with God would be absolute miracles when they come to pass. The faith train is a bare naked surrender to what anyone thinks. It's a constant question of mental health, buckets of tears, and a barrage of begging for a glimpse, as you fight your flesh for instant gratification. God is a God of miracles and fantastic surprises. Wait, it will be awesome. The things we can not see are God's favorite surprises.

When you live by faith, it often feels like you are risking your reputation. You're not, you're risking God's. It's not your faith on the line, it's his faithfulness. Why? Because God is the one who made the promise, and He is the only one that can keep it. - Author unknown

I belong to the church of "sniff your own armpits first before you sniff others" - my mom

I will always risk giving my love rather than be afraid of pain, always.

A person literally only has the power to affect your life as much as you'll let them. If I consistently allow someone to affect my life in a dis-empowering way, then my power, physical mind strength, work, creativity, and dreams are affected. Now tell me, is this truly worth my time? ONLY IF I NEED TO BE RIGHT about the story I made up about why that person affects me negatively. I give up the right to be right!!!!! UNCLE!"

Have you ever pondered the fact that someone you find annoying or hard to be around is being used by the enemy to be annoying? The enemy knows what kind of freedom or truth you have for that person and doesn't want them free. He takes you out instead in your flesh (by being annoyed), not them.

It's always interesting when the blindside is cut away and we are able to see what a small game we were playing. Count it as character building and check out the horizon before you. You have a field to harvest! Lift your eyes up people, take the blinders off, look around there is opportunity everywhere. The enemy has been busy pounding you down. Hell, your own negative self talk is so unacceptable that the enemy can leave you alone for weeks cause you'll take yourself out. This is what I say looking in the mirror at the woman before me. Yeah the beautiful one with gifts and scars and weathering. Perfect.

The grass isn't greener on the other side, it's green where you water, fertilize and care for it

Sometimes life is a blind walk....knowing little ahead....hoping in the promises given....I forge ahead looking for a glimpse of the next thing to stand on.

Being in a state of humble, requires you to not take credit for what God did through you. In fact it should be so good you don't remember it.

God will lift you up so much that you never need to. It's actually pretty funny to watch.

Here's something to ponder: In my relationship with God, I have found that HE does a ton around me all day every day. When I am in the place of actually noticing it, and recognizing HIM, is when real abundance and favor come my way. Why wouldn't he want to do more. If you see Him as a friend, being thankful and telling people what your friend did, would only create a space for your friend to give more in all aspects of your relationship. Gratitude + Recognizing God movement = more favor and abundance.

How much time I have carved out with God is a direct reflection on where I am at physically, emotionally and spiritually. OR in other words, walking in fear or not. Surrounded by drama and responding or grounded in peace. When my identity is in people my life is a train wreck and is an indication it is time to create some connection with God.

"Why are you still single? You are such a fantastic, funny, awesome beautiful woman?"

1.) Do you hear from God? Ask Him and see what He says.

2.) I am choosing to heal, mend, forgive and get whole again and it is a blast.

3.) There hasn't been an offer yet that hasn't made me say in my head "God there has got to be more." "Why do I feel depressed with this effort."

4.) My biological clock is NOT ticking, and therefore I don't feel the pressure to settle just Vto have a baby.

5.) I have yet to be so swept off my feet with a man that has an "A game," can teach me what it's supposed to look like, isn't in it just for his needs or making him feel important, and is ready for the most fantastic relationship of his life.

6.) When I meet him, HE will know it and I will confirm it. I know what I want now and that is worth the wait.

8.) I love hard and with all of my being, and that time will NOT be given to someone whom is looking over their shoulder for someone better.

9.) My man is born, healthy and walking this earth and our paths will cross. That is where flesh and faith align and wait for fantastic, not just ok.

10.) I am absolutely honored to raise two fantastic men whom are without choice, affected by divorce. I will NOT bring in a man to teach them qualities around women that are not commendable, true, honest, and full of grace.

11.) I may lack in faith in this area but God has answered my prayers in so many areas that I will stand strong. I'm ecstatic to meet him and share life with him.

12.) I've finally put a different price tag on myself and it isn't thrift store prices anymore.

13.) I am so interested in the enemy NOT winning with his hideous sentences in between my ears, that I will fight to the death, the death of those sentences and disbelief.

APOLOGY FROM A VERY WHITE WOMAN

How do you honor a man such as Martin Luther King Jr.?

"Faith is taking the first step even when you can't see the whole staircase." MLKJ

I woke up early one morning with the urge to write on the subject of equality. Not even knowing what I would write and yet got chills when I thought of it. My favorite movie is "The Help". If I was born into that decade I would have been "Skeeter," the white girl that writes about "The Help" and their lives and struggles. This movie is such an amazing portrayal of "the truth" that I've seen in awhile. The unacceptable treatment of a human being back then honestly rips me to the core." It is an embarrassment to me personally knowing that my family probably participated in this long ago. Since I love to expose the "truth" I have seen this movie 6 times. Every time I understand a little more and change for the better in my heart. As a Christian I am called to love, period. If that is truly my only task then that should be enough to do for my whole life. As we all get pulled into loss, pain and poor treatment, it always ends in the same question, "Should I love again." MLKJ's love for people, ALL people is something to really ponder. If he, a man on this Earth has that capacity, then quite frankly we all do.

Listen to Just for Today by India Arie – This song inspired me to write this piece.

"Darkness cannot drive out darkness: only light can do that. Hate cannot drive out hate: only love can do that." MLKJ

I am so thankful for the upbringing I had. Honestly, the way we are raised plays a huge part in our attitudes toward man kind. I was taught BY ACTION to love everyone, even my enemies. I was never taught the difference between race. I attended a church where we were the only family without pigment for several years. It was the most real "church" I had experienced till then, talk about mind blowing fun. My mom owned a business with an African American when I was a teen, I graduated from a high school in the heart of Denver where Crips and Bloods (friends of mine) had it out on our front lawn, and spent one eye opening year in Vicksburg, Mississippi where I learned about racial discord. Being from Colorado, I had never understood what racial hatred was about until placed in the heart of hatred. This was in 8th grade and it changed me forever.

"The ultimate measure of a man is not where he stands in moments of comfort and convenience, but where he stands at times of challenge and controversy." MLKJ

When we moved back to Colorado I knew then that I would change hearts even if it was one at a time. As I'm typing this, I get emotional as the flood of amazingly beautiful people cross my mind and path. I can't even imagine my high school years if it were only a sea of white people. We are trained in the striving to be equal to also be PC. There isn't a politically correct bone in my body. I have always seen humor in everyone and all their actions, but mostly mine. I am the one that can say the most un PC statement and the people hearing it KNOW my heart and my LOVE for them. I have quickly bonded with every race because I "poke fun" at the oddities of life. We are all humans that create magic and death all around us. It has nothing to do with skin color. It isn't color of skin I have an issue with, it is character flaws, we are very clear that every human has flaws of character.

I can't even imagine what this world would look like without my incredibly beautifully skinned friends. I can see it now and it makes me wanna crawl back in the womb quite honestly and wait for a better decade. In humor, a sea of pasty white people with red blotchy skin (not that that isn't pretty) doing a dance that looks like Elaine on Seinfeld, listening to mediocre music (probably still Mozart) or one really angry wife beating rapper, and watching sports where no one challenges us to push our bodies to full potential seems pretty close to crapville to me. These are just my thoughts, AND if you know me, you have experienced that I would be miserable in that place. So this blog is to honor and thank God truly for how far equality has come. I am a more beautiful person because of it. I can't imagine it any other way. I can't imagine NOT having the hundreds of friends that don't look like me around. Thank you for giving of yourself to have me in your life. I hope that I have been an asset and impact to you in some way. I owe it all to God and my mother, an amazingly loving woman.

Have we gotten there yet?

"There comes a time when one must take a position that is neither safe, nor political, nor popular, but he must take it because conscience tells him it is right." MLKJ

"There comes a time when silence is betrayal." MLKJ

If you hear anything from this, I want you to hear this. I ask for your forgiveness on behalf of all white men or women for any actions or words that have caused you to feel unequal in this society. I humbly apologize for the continued silent thoughts or verbally abusive comments I hear from the white man. We have come a long way and still have so far to go. Will you accept my apology from this white woman for the disrespect that you have felt. I can't stop any of others actions but I could possibly be the rare find that releases you into a place of personal freedom as you choose to forgive. I have found in life, where I am in extreme judgment it is ALWAYS a mirror of myself and what I dislike about ME. I have often cried after hearing the stories from my closest friends and the words spoken in hatred toward them. I can only pray that that seed grows into amazing fruit that you can take into your generation and your children to teach them LOVE. LOVE for all people no matter what.

"Nothing in the world is more dangerous than sincere ignorance and conscientious stupidity." MLKJ

"I have a dream that my four little children will one day live in a nation where they will not be judged by the color of their skin but by the content of their character." MLKJ

I am so proud to be a part of MLKJ's dream of equality. I have had the honor of having incredible, trustworthy, honest, loving, forgiving, passionate, leaders and friends in my life and most of these amazing people are NOT white. For that I am truly honored.

Please share this on Facebook with someone you would like to honor that isn't your race. That is going to take me awhile today and it is totally worth each life I speak into because we all matter. What a difference we could make in just this one action. It gives me chills. I might not be MLKJ but I have a voice and it could, in today's technology be heard by hundreds of thousands of people.

Have fun blessing and speaking into other's lives today and paying it forward! I know I will.

THE RIPPLE EFFECT

I want to share the comments I received from people who read this. It was one of my most humbling, raw and proud days.

Loved your blog, love you more! Honored to have you in my life, girlie! –Camille W.

A beautiful, heartfelt, inspiring blog from one of my buddies. Thank you Amanda Sharp for shining your light for all of us to share. -Sylvia A.

Dearest Amanda…. words fail me right now, after reading your most inspiring blog. BRAVO!!! I connected deeply with every word you wrote. Thank you, my dear for expressing so beautifully what MANY of us feel. -Unknown

YOU DID IT, SWEETUMS!!! GMA

Amanda……my words cannot express what I feel right now! Thank you… – Lesia B

Nice – keep being you – Rissa L

This took guts to write and send. Thank you for sharing your heart – Lisa M.

I loved reading your blog and you owe no apology for the past. I do accept the notion that we move forward in the spirit of the dreamer and keep the dream alive through true compassion for all people. – Kathy R.

Amanda … enjoyed reading your blog and the quotes of a man (Martin Luther King Jr.) that asked in regards to his funeral…that it not be mentioned that he won a Nobel Peace Prize or received over 300 awards. That he be remembered as a drum major of peace, justice and righteousness. The sad history of mankind is that there has always been slavery . History tells us that so unlike the movies … most slaves that were brought to America were not captured … but were sold into slavery by other tribes. —— Claude H.

So impressed reading of your life and the diverse friendships you have had. I feel that is the great equalizer in mankind learning to love and respect one another. - Unknown

Amanda, my love, you touch my heart yet again in a profound way. Thank you for "Seeing Me." Not many people can do that, even if they say it. You my friend have seen both sides of the picture, not many people have the honor of going there and have the honor of keeping that knowledge and sharing it. The feelings are, can I say, eccentric for lack of better words. It's like being in a room where I am the only one that speaks a different language and not having a soul understand the inner most feelings that are pounding and striving to get out. They can't get out, because there is a strong lack of understanding. The movie, "The Help," sadly is still being portrayed "LIVE" in many states. As I sat in the restroom after seeing this accurate portrayal of "life" behind the eyes of a black woman in the south, I overheard some women from Atlanta saying, "this is still happening right now where I live." That was 2011. But Jesus has sent people who DO indeed get it. The dream lives on… MY DREAM, where all men are created equal and there are no hidden agenda's; where there are no slaves among slaves; and there are no questions about RACE on applications. Yep you can smile on that one. - Debbie C.

Wow. Great words of wisdom. Many do not get it. But you my friend have a good understanding. Race, as I see it, will always play a factor in our lives. With our current POTUS and all that has been said and all that is in print shows how relevant it still is. If we could get more Amandas. Lol. Thank you for your words. They are heart felt and I hope you continue to let your voice be heard. From here to that mountain top Martin was talking about. Raymon W.

This is a very inspirational piece. We have come a long way but it is clearly evident that we have a long way to go. I have faith that we will get there through our children and their children. – Doug H.

This was wonderful to read. Thank you for sharing. – Barbara W.

I agree, I have nothing to apologize for in forward movement as I have lived the dream of equality in my lifetime and am forever grateful to those who have gone before me to make it so. May God give us the courage we need to liberate at ALL times, for ALL people. – Andrea M

Skeeter is my all time hero. "The Help" is my favorite as well. You done good. You is smart, you is good, and you is beautiful. – Kathy H.

Amanda, Amanda, Amanda so powerful and sincere. I want to hug you and hold on! You touched me only where a few people are allowed access! Keep sowing the seed of Beauty… it will indeed change the world! Go Girl! -Kenya T

Thank you Amanda, I love that you spoke from your heart….you are such a gem. We will always have a connection, we are SOUL sisters. :-) Nedra J

Dear Amanda

Thanks for the kind words concerning my mothering abilities and I really enjoyed the quotes from MLKJ. I have never read anything about his life and those quotes got me interested to do so. I share all your emotions and sentiments on the subject of race and I am glad you were so touched by "The Help." That movie was one generation behind mine but as has been mentioned, some things have not changed all that much in the South. I have often thought if the bigots would just shut up for one generation, a lot of bigotry would not be passed forward, but they are often the most vocal and self-righteous. It seems that the kids are doing a better job of "mixing it up" than the adults. Let's remember to support them in their efforts to see each other as individuals, loved by God. Thanks for the blog. Love Mom

You know what Amanda. I myself have never heard a white express herself to me this way. I have always considered you as my sister because we share the blood of Jesus. I am also accustomed to hypocritical fellowship from all of my supposed white Christian sisters due to their lack of repentance from bigotry. The evidence of this is revealed in their behavior as you stated in your blog….hateful comments and racist thoughts manifested through their actions any time they are to be obligated to interact with you; as they are confused on how to handle or accept the forced treatment they continue to endure. There were multitudes of so called Christian slave masters who proudly expressed their superior thoughts in actions rape, lies, theft and murder in more than one race. In this era it is strategically exercised by power of denial. As a knowledgeable black woman myself I refuse to reason with this logic and simply endure my packaged oppression due to serenity.

Anyway I just wanted you to know how much of an impact your letter has made in my spirit. You have canceled a lot of pain within my heart for I cannot deny the sincerity in this blog. Girl you are indeed one of a kind and it is a true blessing to connect with you. Glory to GOD for showin' up and showin' out at this divinely appointed time. You are a refreshment at a time of thirst and I would like to just give thanks unto our mighty Father for your existence. May HE increase you, elevate you and provide you with all you need to do HIS will. You are an example of HIS love and HIS glory. Thank you for being His finger and touching my heart you are truly a rarity. Can't wait to party with you in Heaven.
Apology Accepted – Unknown

Action · Growth · Awareness

1. Listen to <u>Just for Today</u> by India Arie

2. Make a ripple effect on peoples lives. Make a difference. Hear someone. Bless and encourage until you get tired.

3. Journal about what you created after reading this.

4. Take a minute to reflect what you have created with God through this book and pass on the gift.

5. Watch the movie <u>The Help</u>

Journal

Insight • Answers • Downloads
AHA's • Wisdom • Findings

SMALL **TALL** *tales*

JUST PLANE FUN – CONT.

I'M JUDGING YOU AND IT'S KILLING ME

I have been blessed by an answered prayer, where I should set my roots for a church. I found a place that is small and growing quickly because the pastor allows the Holy Spirit to move. Oh how I have missed that. You know the kind where He spends all weekend writing a sermon and then allows (or trusts) God to switch it up on stage in the moment, and let Him talk through him? Or the kind of place where you stand there and feel like your whole heart is going to burst, and the only composure you can muster is looking straight forward with rivers of tears melting away the pain. The bursting is the deep deep love that God has for me. It physically creates lack of breath as I let him in to the deepest darkest rooms. Yes the pain that I have stuffed and stuffed and pulled out when I was ready to heal more.

This pastor is the kind that can "see you" and by that I mean, he is awakened to all senses including fervent prayer warrior. This guy is someone who knows me and doesn't know me at all. In fact, he just shook my hand. That is called a follower of Christ. The one that breathes life into you, just by his beingness and doesn't take credit for what God speaks through him. That to me is the best kind of teacher, truly the only kind I enjoy learning from. Honestly, when it is from God, the flesh and brain are so numbed out that the speaker walks off stage and says "hmmm what did I just say?" When its not full of "self" it is pretty amazing.

Fast forward months later to a service for our brand new building......a Baptist church. As I parked, I thought "no way." A flood of judgment and thoughts rushed through my mind. All past experiences and turn offs I had acquired in my years specifically around Baptists flooded my mind. Really, the judgment were around people and their actions (just to be clear). I walked in and thought this is so God to have us rent space from a Baptist church. Then I thought, wait, they should be meeting on Sunday, what is going on? I was greeted by a fantastic loving woman and chose a seat close up to the front of a huge crowd because I wasn't going to miss this. I sat there as the announcement was made that we had merged with three denominations since I was gone. What? Churches split over the smallest human "need to be right" around doctrine. This was going to be one of the biggest miracles I have seen in my life time. Take a moment to ponder this............I know I did.

If God can bring three churches together, then that must mean ALL miracles were on the table for me. This is what He loves doing. This is His MO, blowing up our small mindedness and unfolding miracles so that we can greatly expand our belief around everything. This is like a live TV reality show! I'm so in. How a group of very different people come together and serve the same God without judgment, just love. It's about mixing us together to give strength to each other's weakness. Not to judge, but to hang around different people in order to make huge character shifts together. To gather together and share of our personal miracles, to encourage each other to move into more, instead of settle for a death oriented and mediocre life. That is church.....I am home.

Listen, when everyone removes resistance, and the need to be right, God can move. God can break out of the box I've put Him in and can be free to do miracles.

The kicker (GET READY FOR GUT LEVEL DISBELIEF): Somehow I must have settled on the fact that religions can't mix. I fully believed that it was impossible to serve God in the same room for extended amounts of time. How have I tossed out hope to come together with others? I'm pretty positive heaven is going to be a mix of all backgrounds with a common belief. I believe my small mindedness mostly came out of feeling inadequate around Bible or religious debates. I never wanted to be challenged on scriptures by an analyst because my experience of that was a total unloving, judgmental space, and one I didn't want to be a part of. I follow God because He is in my life and intricately answers my prayers. The details He orchestrates on my behalf is why I never question God. If you haven't chosen to experience that with God I got nothing to argue with you about or be right about. You just know that you know.

Where else in life have I let the bad judgmental experience of one person create a judgment on ALL of "THOSE PEOPLE." My favorite bumper sticker is "Jesus, save me from your people." Sobering and true. Where have I not allowed relationship with someone because they weren't like me? This was a convicting service to say the least. I could barely stand for praise and worship as it was so draped with God's loving correction. The oldest member was honored that day which was a testament to someone being open to God's movement is possible at that age. Again, not something I had experienced with elderly. Then I scan across the room and there is this man pierced and covered in tats. I saw him get baptized months ago and he now brought a friend to receive what he had from God. Can I get a side order of humble pie please and a case of conviction? This man, was bringing more to Jesus then I had in a year probably. Who am I kidding, when was the last time I lead someone to Christ?

What now? I am wide eyed and open to all God has for me. Every single person has something to offer me. I have a lot of learning to do. I have missed out on relationship. After service I immediately went to hug both of them to honor their hearts and being soft and moldable by God. Lord, help me stay here, it is awesome.

Go out and LOVE..........it will greatly change your whole existence.

1. Listen to <u>Oceans</u> again by Hillsong United

2. How have your judgments stolen relationship from you?

3. What judgment around a religion/s do you have, or is it about the experience or treatment of the person toward you?

4. How much healing can you bring to yourself and others by changing your beliefs around judgment?

5. Send me an email at <u>sharpdesignsinc@mac.com</u>, or on Facebook, and tell me your experience of this journey. It will fuel me more to step into my gifts. Post my link or status feed on Facebook, Twitter, Vine and Insta-gram. Please take a moment to go on to amazon.com and leave a review.

Journal
Insight • Answers • Downloads
AHA's • Wisdom • Findings

Journal

Insight • Answers • Downloads
AHA's • Wisdom • Findings

TESTIMONIALS OF CHARACTER

Below are the people in my life that have been there on part or the whole journey. All of them have been huge support to me finishing this book. I asked them to do a character testimonial in order to highlight them and honor the role they have played in my healing, wisdom & breakthrough. Just knowing what the title was could make any of them wonder how did I mix humor and God. This could be very scary to put your stamp of approval on. With that being said, none of them have read this book before writing their response. All of them trusted my vision.

"If your back was against the wall, you had no hope, no belief in yourself and couldn't see any way to overcome life's greatest obstacles, what would you do? Amanda has been there and through it all she has never lost sight of who her Lord and Savior is and how, through him, she can overcome her greatest challenges. As a single mother, Amanda stood up to that voice that was a constantly telling her she didn't deserve, wasn't good enough, not smart enough, not talented enough, and would never be the woman she was meant to be. And it wasn't easy! There were times when her doubt became so powerful that all she could do was fall on her knees and pray to God that He would lift her back up. And through it all, she found ways to bless others with her wit, humor, laughter and love. She is a prayer warrior that you want on your team. Amanda loves her two boys and sacrifices much to make sure that they grow into men who know how to love themselves, love others and treat women with the greatest respect. Using humor and raw openness, Amanda has written this book so that you too can see the possibility of becoming your authentic self regardless of life's circumstances. I know you will be blessed by Amanda as my family and I have."

John Edwards
Lead Facilitator for Klemmer & Associates
President and CEO, JTM Enterprises, Inc

Amanda and I have been friends literally since we were in diapers. Our Moms met when we were babies and they babysat their girls one for the other within their babysitting co-op. She has a stand out sense of humor and always has a way to look at life in a positive light. Amanda has a knack for making people laugh and is a joy to be around. Amanda has taken hard times and been an example of inspiration, determination and courage. She motivates me to look to God and be strengthened by His Son to navigate through difficult situations. She has much insight and wisdom. Amanda is raising her two boys to love and trust God. Her optimism and dedication to them is obvious.
– Carly Baker

Amanda has been my closest friend for more than 20 years and I GUARANTEE this book will make you laugh, leave you in shock that some of these stories are even true (they are!), and challenge you with a new and deeper perspective of spirituality! Amanda and I have gone through college years, relationships, lives falling apart and coming back together, and faith falling apart and coming back together... sit back with a cup of coffee and enjoy! Scratch that—no cup of coffee unless you want it coming out of your nose!
– Carey Chamberlin

We have known Amanda since she was a baby. She is a very conscientious, organized and also a fun loving person. She has done so much in her life from her many accomplishments to her empathy and caring for other people. Her Christian values show through in all aspects of her life from the way she is raising her boys to her stands in moral issues. She is a wonderful person and we look forward to her book. – Joe & Leeann Focer

One of the first things I noticed about Amanda is her true gift of telling a story so full of emotion, humor and inspiration, that she had a huge room full of people laughing until they cried and crying until they laughed. This is simply who she is. Naturally insightful, kind and hilarious! Amanda shares life lessons, often born of struggle and adversity with such wit that even heavy subjects are much easier to bear. I'm so blessed to know that she is choosing to share this God-given gift on a much larger stage, blessing so many people around the world. Laughter is indeed good medicine! Thank you for the precious gift of your many talents, your support and your unconditional love! In gratitude, Sabrina Desanti

"Be the change that you wish to see in the world." --Mahatma Gandhi
Apparently Amanda Fillweber wishes to see humor, joy and F-U-N in this world. She certainly has brought that and so much more into my life. I'm so anxious to read this book because I know it was written from a place of love, vulnerability and healing. It's heavily seasoned with Amanda's unique sense of humor, which I find sometimes shocking and almost always hysterical!! Amanda does not hide behind her humor. We've shared from our hearts with each other; we've cried together; held each other accountable and encouraged each other. Her openness, honesty and integrity created a space for her in my inner circle. Her sense of humor was the cherry on top. Amanda, I'm so proud of you for stepping into the woman God created you to be. You're a fantastic mom; creative genius; a published author; a trusted and loyal forever friend. I love you! Congrats!

Love, Your Adopted "Mom" – Linda Edwards

I have known Amanda since 2008? We have always been very real, very deep and spiritual and very funny with each other. A couple of years after we met, Amanda and I each experienced excruciatingly painful losses. We have walked the road of shock, grief, anger and healing together and continue to "do life" together regularly. I have seen so much growth in this dear friend. She has always been a safe place to share even my ugly side without judgment or condemnation. She has trusted God when fear was crouching at her door and a mountain of uncertainties was before her, she has chosen to extend grace many times when "getting even" would have seemed just. More than anything else that I appreciate in Amanda is how she has loved God, learned to love herself with Grace, loved her sons and loved me.

I love you my dear friend, Susie Martin

Amanda Fillweber is a filthy hilarious, God fearing woman. How those two things get wrapped into one unique package is shocking to me too. One of my favorite things about her is you never know what will come out of her mouth, and just when I think I do, something even funnier does. She is a loving mother, creative photographer and all around great friend. She is the shoulder you can cry on, and know she will say something sarcastic enough to help you laugh your tears away. Or just laugh so hard you cry. Her writing is an opportunity to crawl into her brain and see how all of the unique puzzle pieces of her brain fit together to create something heavy, deep and real funny.

Krystal Zellmer - Facilitator for Klemmer & Associates

Amanda is someone who does what she says she will do. She may resist in the beginning of her process and yet when she digs deep she takes on the challenge with her full heart. Why would you want to read this book? Because Amanda uses comedy through chaos and finds a way to make it all work out. She pushes herself to go beyond what others think is the limit. We all go through challenges and our attitude is a big part of getting through those challenges. Amanda takes that too a whole new level. You will laugh and cry and remind yourself that you too can get through the challenges. I have had the opportunity to coach Amanda on how to get herself out of debt so she can focus on what she is called to do. As the author of "Welfare to Wealth" I know that it takes commitment, perseverance and lightening up to get through the tough situations we face. When helping women through the coaching and consulting I provide, they step up and build what is in the heart. Amanda is a great example of stepping up and taking action on what has been in her heart and I am sure you will see how you can too!

Kimberley Borgens
CBC is the CEO of Be A Legacy.
Known as the "Queen of Accountability" because she holds women accountable to what they say they want in life. Mega-entrepreneur with five different thriving businesses Kimberley speaks and works with women in business and in direct sales on creating an action plan for success and build the quality support needed to be successful long term. Contact Kimberley at dreamteam@bealegacy.com or visit the website and discover more www.bealegacy.com

'Laughter is like a good medicine.' Amanda embodies this truth. Even in deep personal loss and disappointment, her character and humor have grown and flourished. This book is a glimpse into who she truly is.

Teresa Martin
CTA Certified Coach
teresamartin6@yahoo.ca
www.teresa-martin.com

I love to read anything Amanda writes. Not only is she witty and authentic, she can also reach in and grab your heart at any moment. Her love for her fellow human beings is felt at a level that is missing in the world today. Amanda brings joy, peace and laughter to anyone reading her work. I can never just read a line or two!

Dr. Angi Moormann
Naturopath, CNHP, Microscopist,
GAPS Practitioner,Life Coach

Have you read a book or talked to someone and said, "ok that was nice but it does not seem real or applicable to me". Well Amanda is real. She will tell you how it is and walk you through life's journey offering her experiences, her losses and her friendship. She is a great guide to when the chips are down, how we can crawl into our Father's lap and be comforted in his grace. She is an inspiration and a dear friend to so many. I am blessed to be one of them.

Brian & Roxanne Fitzgerald - CRM, CIC, AIC
CEO and President of Colorado Lifestyle

Amanda's deep, raw and honest examination of life's triumphs, tragedies, family and faith, typically has us either laughing, sobbing, or both at the same time. She hits the emotional "hot button" on subjects many authors only mention (or avoid altogether) with an authentic passion, vulnerability and a healthy dose of humor. An engaged reader can't avoid honestly examining their own behavior, motives, beliefs and emotions while riding this roller coaster of life's questions and experiences with Amanda. Buckle your seatbelt for a FUN reading experience!

Bill & Kathy Hellwig
Executives, Miracles Happen 4U

You should only read Amanda's writing if you want to laugh, want to be exposed to the truth, the whole truth, and nothing but The Truth. She pours out of her life lessons and blesses you with life application. She does so with humor, grace, love and even more humor. She leads her readers to lean into their faith as the foundation for daily life and she does this from a place of absolute encouragement and never with condemnation or a pointed finger. Only read Amanda's words if you are ready to shift your life into more and better. She will bless you immensely if you are ready to be changed. If you don't laugh while you read, you might be sleeping!

Jenny Bolt Price
John Maxwell Certified Coach
blogger@iwokeupyesterday.com
Author of 7 Shifts
Headmaster of Klemmer Coaching Academy

Amanda is a very deep well of love, compassion, faith and humor. She is able to put this recipe in the right order at the right time for all that share space with her. If Amanda was at the last supper, she'd whoopie cushion Jesus just to release the pressure in the room. – Cory King

My experience of Amanda is of a loving mother, caring friend, and pee your pants laughing hilarious Christian woman. She has this amazing ability to connect with people through her humor and she shares her faith and love of God in such an accepting, non judgmental way. This woman day in and day out is finding the funny side of life. No matter how tough the situation she cracks me up with her jokes, pictures, and life stories. She's an inspiration to me to celebrate the greatness (and the funny stuff) in my life. I totally trust that the messages that Amanda is sharing in this book will be an gift to all those who read it. - Jenna Ziegler, RN, BSCN

I first knew Amanda as the photographer of the event I was attending. But she was more than that, she was an encourager. As I worked to conquer a task bigger than I had ever imagined, I could hear her voice as she shouted words of encouragement, telling me how awesome I was and that I could do it. Weeks later I contacted Amanda to ask her for some advice regarding my photography business. What I heard from Amanda was, once again, encouragement. To take on the world. To not compare myself to others. But more clearly, the most important message, to trust a God that is bigger than I could ever imagine. Amanda has become a coach, friend, and mentor to not just me, but all who she "loves" on. (Her words.) She has helped me understand what it means to live an abundant, Christ-centered life. She has seen things in me that I haven't seen in myself. Her teachings through her humor have helped me to grow into a courageous, worthy woman who has begun to truly believe in her power. I'm 100% positive that if you asked 100 people who have had the opportunity to be with Amanda for anytime at all, they will tell you that she has affected their life in the most positive way. I feel truly blessed to have been the recipient of such a great gift in my life. – Roni Rumsey

Amanda's writings are overflowing with love, wisdom, and humor. Her real life experience with tragedy, faith, hope, and transformation is a true blessing. – Jamie Rauch, CEO

Amanda is straight forward, honest, and funny. She has walked through a wide variety of life experiences, which has molded her into the wise, empathetic, and God-trusting woman she is today. She has spent time reflecting and living through her experiences in such a way that she can relate to and support others through their tough times as well. Her book is sure to be a fun, memorable, and an impactful read. – Carolyn Stokes

Amanda is the real deal and she has a passion for life and laughter second to none. I had the privilege of reading one page of this book and I am hooked. Amanda writes in a humorous yet thought provoking style that will captivate you on page one. This book is a must read. You will laugh and you will cry as Amanda shares her journey through the joy and pain in her life. No matter what storm she was facing, Amanda weathered it with strength and integrity, standing firm in her faith and laughing in the face of the enemy. Heavy Deep and Real Funny should be a book on everyone's coffee table.

John & Rita Ziehr
john@marriageconnect.org
www.marriageconnect.org
Chiropractor with advance certification in Neuro-Emotional Technique (NET) Ordained minister for 22 years. Rita has a passion to lead women to emotional health and wholeness.

In "Daring Greatly," Brene Brown writes: *Don't squander joy. We can't prepare for tragedy and loss. When we turn every opportunity to feel joy into a test drive for despair, we actually diminish our resilience. Yes, softening into joy is uncomfortable. Yes, it's scary. Yes, it's vulnerable. But every time we allow ourselves to lean into joy and give in to those moments, we build resilience and we cultivate hope. The joy becomes a part of who we are, and when bad things happen-and they do happen-we are stronger.*

Heavy, Deep, and Real Funny does just that. Reading through as one of her editors, Amanda provides us with a tool that allows us to make joy a part of us. Amanda takes you on a journey that is both humorous, soul-searching and refreshing. Her action steps are easily doable and at the same time life-altering. She shares her heart and her soul with you with tons of water-spewing-out-of-your-nose laughs. This is one of those books where you learn to expect the unexpected. Amanda has the gift of using the funny instances in life and take them deeper. It's not just the surface stuff; it's digging deep down and releasing some of the junk that we tend to carry, with humor and style. Amanda's wit and vulnerability are humbling and this book is such a gift. Why not give it a peek, laugh out loud, and gain a new perspective on life? If you're looking for the tools to break-through along with laughs that come from the heart, this is the book for you.

Destiny DeHaven
Klemmer & Associates Certified Coach
B.A.N.K. PhD
www.LoveCommunicates.com
www.playbankcode.com/itsdestiny

IN MEMORY OF
JENNY BERLIN GALE – JUNE 12, 2014

Jen worked at School of Mines as a professor in the English Department and couldn't wait to edit my book. We talked many times about what we were writing about. She had quite a few writing projects going as well. We laughed no matter what topic we were discussing. We talked about God a ton. It's intimate to share those conversations when someone is fighting cancer raging through their body. She was at peace again with HIM. Honestly the time I shared with Jen about God might be the most proud time of my life. I know where you are and I feel you laughing with me often.

She passed away a couple months before I got my book to her. She fought against numerous brain tumors and they won. Her spirit was hopeful and she was a fighter. She took on things personally that most would quit on. She was a lover of people and always gave of herself. I am honored to call her my sister and I deeply miss her. I was with her during her last days where all I could do was cry and hold her warm hand. If you've ever watched someone leave this earth then you know how heart wrenching this is, especially when they don't respond.

Jen, I am inspired to finish this book because you were one of my biggest fans. I love you and I still hear your laugh and playfulness. Thank you for believing in me. This one's for you babe, it's heavy, deep and real funny. Just like us.

One of her notes to me on my blog: journeytoourlegacy.wordpress.com

You know I love you so much and you are my inspiration! There are paths that we don't share in this journey, but I am your number one supporter in your bravery, willingness to share, and awareness of issues that touch us all deeply. I will gladly help you in any cause you choose to pursue. Oh, did I mention humor? Love it, love you, thank you for being so brave, shows me maybe someday I can be too! – Jenny G.

ABOUT THE AUTHOR

Amanda currently resides in Colorado Springs, Colorado where she raises to gorgeous, fun and witty boys. She is a graduate of Oral Roberts University, an NCAA Volleyball player, has a degree in Graphic Design and is the President of Sharp Designs, Inc where she has captured photography since 1995. She is also a business mentor with a nutrition company since 2007. She is an amazingly creative woman and loves all aspects of being an artist. She is not a religious woman, she is just real about her trials and successes. They all include God. She would love to create relationship with you and thanks you for taking a journey with her in this book. She strongly believes she is just a messenger and allows God to write through her. She hopes you are blessed by the gentleman, her intimate friend, Jesus (not the Hispanic one). It has taken her ten years to get this book written because her desire to not grieve Him was important. She finally came to the "Grace Room" and got numerous direct confirmations that it was time. Sit back, surrender and just create a freedom journey only you can.

You can follow her on Facebook, Twitter (sharptweetinit), Linkedin,
Vine (heavydeepandrealfunny),sharpdesigns.isagenix.com, Instagram (sharpdesigns)
and email sharpdesignsinc@mac.com.

Journal

Insight • Answers • Downloads
AHA's • Wisdom • Findings

Journal
Insight • Answers • Downloads
AHA's • Wisdom • Findings

Made in the USA
Monee, IL
21 March 2021